IN
OBSCURA

PART I

IN OBSCURA

PART I

Peter Theroux

STATION
SQUARE
MEDIA
NEW YORK, NEW YORK

In Obscura
Adventures in the World of Intelligence, Part One

Published by Station Square Media

Editorial and Production Director: Janet Spencer King
Cover/Interior Design: Steve Plummer, SP Design

Printed in the United States of America for Worldwide Distribution
ISBN: 979-8-9904497-0-1

Electronic Edition
ISBN 979-8-9904497-1-8

*Note: The first chapter in this book, "I Hate My Boss,"
originally appeared in a different form in Tablet magazine (TabletMag.com) and is reprinted with permission.*

THE TITLE IS an old CIA operational term from Latin referring to the status of clandestine work, literally in the dark. An intelligence officer engaging in espionage who has successfully evaded enemy surveillance so that he can commit an operational act is said to be "black" or "IO"—*In Obscura.*

Lynda Obst's memoir *Hello, He Lied, and Other Takes from the Hollywood Trenches* inspired this project of mine. The year before I left Los Angeles to join government service, she published her page-turner about how movies are made without sensationalism or score-settling. ("This is not a mean book," she wrote in the preface, "so if that's what you seek, seek elsewhere.") Much as Hollywood books skew towards glamour and character assassination, the CIA genre skews heavily disgruntled, partisan, axe-grinding, and self-aggrandizing. Obst wrote an enthralling insider account for movie lovers about what producers, directors, agents, writers, actors, casting and location scouts, hair, makeup, wardrobe, and film editors do all day to get movies made. I decided the cast of the intelligence world—analysts, targeters, case officers, upper management—merits the same kind of effort.

A stark difference is that I must abide by secrecy agreements. I can't drop some of the names I'd like to, let alone "tell all." "Tell as little as possible" isn't the sexiest way to start a book, at least in Part One. At the time of writing, I still hold a top secret clearance, and the US government imposes a rule that in addition to not revealing classified information, I am held to the standard of a current, full-time, overt employee and therefore may not publish views that might suggest partisanship or judgments that could lead a foreign ally to conclude that there is unfair bias at work. Nor may I undermine current USG policies.

I will have my clearance vacated before writing Part Two, which finishes the job of detailing my intelligence career and a few family issues. And by then, I ought to be able to say, along with John Ray Jr., Ph.D (the fictional author of the foreword to Nabokov's *Lolita)* that, "the caretakers of the various cemeteries involved report that no ghosts walk."

But here we are.

Contents

The monument to Basil al-Asad, Qardaha,
Syria. The playboy "martyr" gallops to heaven,
spurred by the prayers of the murderous
President Hafez al-Asad below.

I Hate My Boss

ONE CONGENIAL DAY in Damascus in 1994, as we shared a flask of arak, the Arab novelist Abdelrahman Munif and I got on to the topic of the pains of leading a double life under an unnatural regime. Speaking very softly, he told me about a hunting trip he had recently taken in south-western Syria with his friend Hamza al-Barqawi, in the wild desert outside Suwayda, and how when their conversation turned to domestic politics, they found themselves moving closer to each other and speaking in near-whispers, before coming to themselves and chuckling at these insecure instincts. But even then, they did not risk raising their voices when discussing the Assad family dictatorship.

"We're trained," Munif told me sadly. "It's an unbreakable habit with us."

I understood. Earlier that same late summer day, I had taken a poolside break from fieldwork for a National Geographic article on Syria at Le Méridien Hotel-Damas. I had my little Grundig Yacht Boy short wave radio tuned to Israel Army Radio, with perfect reception—over that same stretch of southern Syria—via a discreet plug in one ear. The whole time, I was ostentatiously perusing one of Syria's unreadable regime newspapers, probably *al-Baath*, for deflection.

The following night, my training in practiced discretion intruded on my peace of mind in Munif's company. I had joined him and his wife at the bright and commodious apartment of the painter Nazir Nabaa and his wife in central Damascus, off leafy Abu Rummaneh Street, not far from the US ambassador's residence. After a few cocktails, Nabaa showed us some of his recent paintings, then proudly led everyone down a hallway to see a couple of works loaned by everyone's mutual friend Marwan—this was Marwan Kassab-Bashi, a celebrated Damascene then residing in Berlin.

"This is a series," said Nabaa, gesturing towards a series of works, the first of which showed a row of young males seen in silhouette and slightly from below, facing the viewer, looking lost. It was skillfully done; as the figures challenged or appealed to you, their round solemn heads and expressive limbs hanging at their sides showed the influence of the French artist Balthus. Nabaa went on to explain that these young men were the *ashbâl* (lion cubs) who had "slaughtered the Zionists in Munich."

"The *fedayeen*, from the Olympiad," his wife clarified approvingly.

"Here is another version," said Nabaa, drawing our attention to a similar but less finished work, a study done in charcoal, and a third, a study of the face of one of the young murderers. "He was martyred, you know. They were all martyred," he said, looking straight at me.

These were the Black September terrorists who had kidnapped, tortured, and murdered eleven Israeli wrestlers and their coaches at the 1968 Munich Olympics, and I was being invited by a roomful of writers and art lovers to accept all this—this violence, terrorism, and Jew-hatred—in the name of hospitality, because I was twice a guest, first Munif's, and also Nabaa's, on this night out. Was this a test, an insult, or a non-event to them?

At one level, this was little different from the daily discomfort endemic for visitors to any dictatorship where they don't want to appear rude or complicit. Damascus was particularly tricky—as of that year, it hosted not only a dozen Arab terrorist and violent dissident groups, but the world's most senior extant Nazi, Alois Brunner, rumored to live on nearby Abd al-Malik Street and whose last sighting would be at the same Méridien where I was staying, only about one year later. The Syrian regime had always been a lavish murderer of its own people, and I knew enough to separate the regime from ordinary Syrians, who tended to be delightful artisans, cooks, and storytellers. But Nabaa's show of these Kassab-Bashi paintings had led me into a penumbra where art, cocktail drinkers, and regime ideology intersected. Perhaps I was not alone in my discomfort. Heck, it was only the previous day that Munif had shared his thoughts on the hardships of where and when one might say things out loud.

I wanted to tell Nabaa that in conventional terms, martyrs were men and women who led lives of heroic virtue and lost their lives to pagans or tyrants of history. Terrorists who murdered defenseless athletes and then got shot by the police were something entirely different. How boxed in should I feel in this pro-Moscow city, driven here and soon to be driven home by a close friend of Nabaa and Marwan? How outspoken might I be for basic decency?

"Marwan is great," I ventured. "In his artistic skill, but martyrdom is a funny thing here, *chez vous*."

No matter that Nabaa gave me exactly the quizzical look I expected or that, later on, the drive back to drop me off at the hotel was awkward, partially because I was preoccupied by two thoughts: I probably needed a new line of work, and I must never come back to Baathist Syria, because it felt uniquely shaming. Living in Egypt as a student in the late 1970s had meant worrying about traffic accidents, pollution, and pickpockets, but not violence, and it certainly was no weight on my conscience. Jordan was an easier place to be, and Israel? Easier yet. I had made only short visits to Iraq but immediately and deeply sensed the depression and tyranny affecting people in Baghdad and Karbala. Syria, on the other hand, although one of the most expansive and historically enthralling countries I knew, evinced a unique menace and horror to anyone used to kindly Middle Easterners, especially the gregarious Egyptians and upbeat Israelis. Syrians, by comparison, avoided Westerners and stuck to the party line when they couldn't.

Thanks to all this regional travel, I was already closing in on an informal rule of CIA operatives I would be taught later: "Never go against your gut." While Egyptian plainclothes police were everywhere, they did seem protective, not malevolent; even a graduate student could see that. Jordan was not much different. Iraqis lived in fear, and everyone knew why because its Baathists tortured dissidents and had attempted genocide. Syria, by contrast, pretended to be an oasis of Old World tourism, mostly for Europeans visiting Palmyra, Ugarit, and the biblical sites, and yet in Damascus—with the draw of being the world's oldest continually inhabited city (though Aleppo and Jericho begged to disagree)—the hotel lobbies were full of middle-aged men in leather jackets doing nothing but surveillance, and the normal pedestrians were fearful of eye contact—this was the opposite of young Cairenes, who aggressively engaged foreigners in conversation, asking the time or where you were from; whether English students, pickpockets, or benign, underemployed loafers. The surveillance in Syria exemplified something different and alien, something Soviet. The Ba'ath Party ran a predatory regime, and its people were the prey. Unlike the radical regimes in Algeria, Libya, Iraq, and Iran—whose remoteness from Israel concealed some of their anti-Jewish barbarity—Syria's Golan frontier made it a frontline state in the Mideast conflict, and so its intermittent diplomatic engagements with Jerusalem gave it the veneer of a rational diplomatic player, which obscured its identity as a state sponsor of terrorism second only to Iran.

I was fortunate to enjoy a domestic version of Damascus. As a socialist and native Saudi whom Riyadh had stripped of his nationality due to his anti-monarchist views, Munif was the safest of contacts in Baathist Syria. His family's apartment, adorned with paintings by Kassab-Bashi and Dia al-Azzawi, lay in the western suburb of al-Mezze, on the road to the military airport and adjacent to the Iranian Cultural Center, a fact which his teenage sons and daughters despised. "Look at that!" they would gasp, pointing to the hijab-clad toddlers led by their parents' hands around the Center's grounds. "Muslim girls veil at puberty. So what do those hijabs mean? That they see three-year-old girls as sexual objects!" I, meanwhile, was led into the secular Munif home to the traditional pre-luncheon welcome of "whiskey or arak?" Lunch itself included a green salad bejeweled with pomegranate seeds, pistachio nuts, and chopped avocados.

The Nabaas lived in a wealthy downtown neighborhood between the popular Snack 24 and Sahet al-Marjeh, the plaza by the Old City where the famous Israeli spy Eli Cohen was hanged. The modern Levant being largely unforested, wood tended to be scarce except for mosaic furniture or inlaid backgammon sets. Syrian homes were much more about stone: terrazzo floors, basalt, and limestone walls and arches.

It was within the calcite purlieus of the Nabaa home that Salim, Munif's nephew, once recounted his recent night shift at University Hospital in the early winter of 1994, when the corpse of the presidential son Bassel al-Asaad arrived, shattered by a car accident. His team had barely pronounced the death of Hafez al-Assad's presumptive heir when word of the senior Assad's arrival was announced. Hospital management implored them to do everything possible to make Bassel's smashed head as presentable as possible to allay the dictator's shock.

Salim's story was met with tactful silence, which contrasted with the chatty glee with which I would hear Bassel al-Assad's death described in Hama, a city victimized by Assad regime massacres and rapes. "Bassel's death was like divine vengeance," I was assured by two young fellows entirely lacking in Munif's and Barqawi's discretion. "We all celebrate the anniversary—especially the women."

On a happier note, I could look forward to a translation conference held in wholesome Salt Lake City in the fall of 1995, where I could network for domestic translation and interpretation work that did not involve ... *this*. Did I indeed need a new line of work? I was leaning towards yes. This visit to Syria felt like strike one against the idiot boss: self-employed me.

Yet I was back there a few months later to finish my fieldwork and managed to navigate my way around most of the country without too much interference. By now, I was a known quantity to officialdom, and dutifully reported my presence to the local police, according to the terms of my journalist visa, as I moved from Damascus up through Homs, Hama, the Crusader castles, the Alawite mountains, Aleppo, Palmyra, Doura Europos, and then down to the Golan Heights.

The Golan Heights was Syria's most sensitive border— the one with Israel. To the west and north, the Lebanese and Turkish borders were easy, and to the east, the Iraqi border was tightly monitored but grudgingly open. (In the mid-1990s, Syria and Iraq were not at war but feuding, as pro-Iran Syria had done its utmost during the eight-year Iran-Iraq war to undermine Iraq.) The southern border was closed and sealed with a minefield, and Syrian propaganda rarely even called Israel by its name, preferring Occupied Palestine, the Zionist Entity, or the Zionist Usurping Power. Like Allah, Israel seemed to have ninety-nine names, and none of them flattering, which was the conventional overkill of Syria's virile propaganda, in quaint contrast to its military failures against the country even as its Iranian patron called it by its right name, for the simplicity of the slogan "Death to Israel."

For the Syrian regime, the ironic crown jewel of the unoccupied Golan is the demolished city of Quneitra, dynamited by the Israelis as they withdrew from enemy territory in 1973 at the conclusion of the Yom Kippur War. The homes and houses of worship were all in ruins, as was the once-elegant Shams Cinema. The Syrians never rebuilt the town, preferring to keep it as a political tourist exhibition of Israeli spite. A smarter regime would have rebuilt it and brought back its people to show resilience, but the Syrian regime opted for the Palestinian model of enshrining and perpetuating victimhood.

The Damascus rule was that I could not visit Quneitra without a government escort. And so they imposed upon me a Tony Shalhoub-lookalike minder named Abu Ahmad, who showed up in front of my hotel that morning with a van and driver. We motored south from the capital on Route 7 in his van, stopping in the village of Beit Jinn to buy apples and then through the remotest part of southern Syria to the rising, scenic Golan, breezing through regime and UN checkpoints as Abu Ahmad flashed his ministerial credentials. We parked outside Quneitra and toured the empty streets of the ruined town on foot, gazing up at snowy Mount Hermon to the west and south into Israel, where jeeps busily patrolled the east-west frontier road. I interviewed an elderly married couple, former residents of the town, who had suddenly emerged from a van like ours. We watched twenty or so Druze villagers shout across the two-hundred-meter-wide minefield into the town of Majdal Shams within the Israeli line, using loudspeakers, to trade gossip and family news over what was famously called the Wadi al-Surakh or Shouting Valley. I later learned that the aged couple were full-time employees of the regime's Ministry of Information, whistled up to recite their story of displacement as needed for American, European, North Korean, Iranian, and other media, along with their hopes to return—ludicrous, given the regime's policy never to rebuild. As a Californian familiar with Disneyland, I saw them less as credible sources than as theme park characters at the popular Quneitra Land attraction, but I could not express such a cynical thought in a National Geographic article, let alone to Abu Ahmad.

The job done, in the late afternoon, we turned north back to Damascus via Route 7's green hills as Abu Ahmad embarked upon an increasingly less subtle shakedown routine. It was a weekend day, he reminded me, and he should have been with his family and not on the job, yet he had arranged for the van and given up his day off, so he wanted a hundred US dollars. I reminded him that I had never asked for his help and that he had imposed all this on me; wasn't the van government-supplied, or if it was out of his own pocket, shouldn't he be billing his own ministry? He sparred over how much time I had spent down in Quneitra, the Shouting Valley, and talking to the old geezers when he had family members to take care of. Clearly, implicitly, I thought, the time we had spent with the elderly refugees and watching the Golani Druze shouting over their valley had been an even bigger farce and waste of time to him than it was to me.

If this had been a carpet bazaar in Aleppo or Damascus, our sparring over payment might have made for a colorful anecdote in the article. I was one of thousands of reporters who had visited Quneitra to see and dutifully report all the obvious ruinous details, but the impoverishment and corruption of my government minder, a more revealing story, belonged in the back channel of my expense report, not in the published story. If I wrote truthfully about Abu Ahmad, National Geographic might lose access to Syria. Just as viewing Arab art was one thing but exposing its moral ugliness would cross a line. In my later career, I would remember this as an introduction to managing information that belonged in front channels, back channels, and undisseminated operational channels.

I had experienced something similar not that long before in Egypt, but on a truly Egyptian eighth-wonder-of-the-word scale compared to drab Syria. For National Geographic, Syria amounted to a sort of suburb of western culture, drawing few tourists apart from the biblical-minded Europeans and Iranian pilgrims to its Shia Muslim sites. The magazine covered it perhaps every twenty years. Egypt, on the other hand, was one of the world's oldest and grandest nation-states, a miracle of preserved ancient treasures, and host to ongoing, major archaeological explorations. The country's archaeological glories were frequently featured on the magazine's cover and were the subjects of some of the Society's sumptuous coffee table books. Cairo's cultural officials and diplomats in Washington DC were among the Geographic's coziest contacts.

"Egypt is a minefield, like China," my editors had cautioned me. The host government authorities in both countries tried to shadow and micromanage writers and photographers for the duration of their assignments. This was just the price of doing business, since subscribers loved reading about these two countries. The two governments were obsessive about their image, I was told, for reasons of tourism and the economy generally, along with their overweening national chauvinism. The Cairo government craved magazine coverage with cover art confined to King Tutankhamen's golden funeral mask, as the Chinese wished to be seen as the land of the Great Wall, terra cotta warriors, and magnificent dam projects, omitting the present and their last several decades of mismanagement and repression.

Air and water pollution in Egypt were two themes of the assignment I was working on. I knew from my time there as a student that the magnificent Nile was also the lavish abode of live rats and dead donkeys, as well as of pesticides and chemical fertilizers leaching into it from hundreds of miles of bordering farmland as it flowed to Lower Egypt and into the Mediterranean Sea.

"Pollution is a sign of human activity, a sign that Egypt is flourishing," a senior environmental official explained to me before declining to answer any more questions. His point was especially striking because, that very morning, a spokesman for the highly polluting Helwan cement plant on Cairo's southern edge had informed me that "Pollution is a sign of human activity; this is a great city!" The following day, a deputy mayor of Cairo would share the identical insight, verbatim, though having unburdened himself of the insight, he at least was more talkative than the others, going on to ask, "Why don't you go home and write about air pollution in Los Angeles?"

Eventually, I was able to address pollution in the article because Egyptian professors and scientists appeared not to follow scripts from the Ministry of Information, though it was frustrating that I could not make Cairo's bureaucrats look like jackasses by quoting them accurately.

And then there was Rawia, the gold-bedecked Ministry of Information official who stood out for her fierce protectiveness of Egypt's cultural heritage by icily reminding me that "We come from pharaohs—we are not Arabs!" She also decreed that my forays into the suburb of Imbaba, rumored to be a stronghold of Muslim extremists, were unacceptable. (So, they were surveilling me—I was on foot and using taxis, not using a driver who could rat out my movements.) In her calmer moods, Rawia's favorite topic was her American green card and her intention to go back to Arkansas to complete her master's degree so that she could settle in the US for good. I did not begrudge her preference for the US over Egypt but found it extra irritating to be bossed around by an Egyptian nationalist who, off the record, could not wait to get out of the place. Rawia's yearning to get out of Egypt, like Abu Ahmad's cynicism, would break the fourth wall of the little cultural journalism drama. Strike two.

Of course, the Bible lands were not responsible for all of the little irritations of my chosen career. Back in LA, I had become fascinated not only by the television series *Twin Peaks* but by the workplaces the Los Angeles Times newspaper critic referred to when writing things like, "Office water coolers this week are busier than ever, as viewers try to figure out what the *hell* went on in last night's episode." I pined for colleagues and water coolers—to dissect Lynch's unsettling TV series and to josh each other, and for consistency, instead of this cycle of spending a few weeks in chaotic Middle Eastern cities followed by solitary months spent writing it up.

In the meantime, after a brief stop in LA after returning from Damascus, I did attend the conference in Salt Lake City, weary from jetlag but excited at the thought of new and different opportunities. Attending seminars on handling audiovisual projects, dubbing or subtitling movies, and consecutive court interpretation in the sparkling Red Lion Hotel without being tailed or scolded by snappish foreign officials filled me with joy. Amid the hundreds of stalls at the job fair, I collected brochures from software companies, translation agencies, something called the Joint Publication Research Service, and even the FBI, whose representative asked my age (mid-thirties) and portentously informed me that I could still be an FBI Special Agent, though the cutoff was age thirty-seven. "You're not getting any younger!" the Bureau grandma crowed.

My last memory of the conference was of the late-afternoon event hosted by AT&T Language Line in a suite a few floors above the conference ballrooms. I filed into the suite amid a throng of distinguished literary translators, professors of literature, and every species of expert freelancer, chatting cordially about our respective projects and world travels. At the sight of buffet tables laden with cheese, crackers, mini-quiches, and even chicken wings with tangy sauces, however, all pretense of professional comity vanished. The prospect of free snacks galvanized the dozens of savants to swarm the tables like rapacious crocodiles or Africanized bees on the then-nascent National Geographic Channel. Many started at the closest end of the tables, far from the stacks of small plates, linen napkins, and silverware the food and beverage staff had supplied at the opposite end, but undeterred, attendees stuffed their faces and pockets with all the delicacies they could seize with their bare hands. The corporation's keynote speaker smiled a little ruefully from her podium, commanding almost no attention in the room until the feeding frenzy abated about twenty minutes later.

Just as a man who is his own lawyer has a fool for his client, I had a fool for a boss. This felt like strike three. I needed a new line of work.

Will Rogers Park on Sunset Boulevard welcomes visitors
to the Beverly Hills Hotel across the street.

Leaving LA

The human embryo is curled up in a ball
with the nostrils placed between the two
knees. At death the pupil opens wide.

BEFORE I WAS strapped in with black bands across my chest, waist, and arms, with a little Velcro band tight around one finger, the informal part of the polygraph examination began, but I could not clear out of my head the book I had been reading on the flight that had brought me here from Los Angeles. There are all kinds of advice for those who have to take a lie detector test, and most of it involves not letting the examiner get inside your head.

None of them tell you not to let James Purdy get inside your head. The quote above is from the first page of Purdy's enthralling snuff novel, *Narrow Rooms.*

It was a bright, cold afternoon outside, but I was in a windowless room near the Baltimore/Washington airport where I had been courteously seated by the polygrapher, a kindly Alabamian who duly explained the process and laid out the questions he was about to ask me. Had I ever been convicted of a crime? Had I committed any crime for which I had not been arrested? Had I compromised classified information? There were about a dozen of these.

"Needless to say, as a civilian, I have never even been exposed to information marked 'Classified,'" I told him.

"Maybe because there is no such thing as information marked 'Classified,'" he answered. "There is Unclassified, Confidential, Secret, and Top Secret. That's it. Hollywood invented the big red 'Classified' rubber stamp."

"Well, to be clear, I have never seen any of those, so I have never had access to any of those or compromised, or stolen, or shared them," I said.

"I will want yes or no answers," he replied.

"No."

"Look," he said. "You can tell me anything now, and it's fine. Tell me the truth now—just tell me the truth— and we're good. But if you withhold information from me now, which comes out when I've strapped you in, that's troublesome. Do you understand?"

This polygraph exam was shaping up to be the kind

veterans call a fistfight or a barbecue. Despite my lack of guile and his initial courtesy, we were wary of each other, and I had the feeling he was trying to intimidate and manipulate me. After I was strapped in, he sparred with me on every question despite my nearly pathetic innocence. In addition to the initial questions, "of course I had never been a communist, or a terrorist, or helped or funded either of these or other groups to harm the interests of the United States, or those seeking to assist them." His close observation was trained not on me but on what he called his "instrument," except when he barked at me to stop moving my foot and accused me of breathing at half the rate I had been breathing before he had strapped me in. While I had been examining my conscience, he had been counting my inhalations.

At one point, the examiner turned the instrument off and took a few moments to sit back and talk about the moment to build rapport and to emphasize how solidly he was on my side. Clearly, I was an intelligent young man, the exact kind of young man the US government needed. He smiled kindly. I had passed an atrocious Arabic exam, right? So this should be easy. Why wasn't it?

It should have been. The language exam earlier that day and a separate code-breaking exam based entirely on a made-up language had been so enjoyable that I could have taken them all day. The Arabic listening exam was heaven: airborne pilots' dialogue with each other; slang in various dialects; the terse recitations of Syrian and Iraqi news anchors. I had, as it turned out, scored high on the exam and anticipated the *Fail Safe* dream of my boyhood hero, Peter Buck, whose ease with innumerable dialects of hard languages had earned him the praise of the fictitious president; Buck was played by Larry Hagman with Henry Fonda as the (unnamed but Kennedyesque) commander-in-chief in the 1964 movie adaptation.

A few days later, aboard United Airlines flight 947, en route from Washington DC to Los Angeles, the evening of Thursday, January 25, 1996, I was enjoying more than the usual mental confusion. This was the ride home from those few days mostly in suburban Maryland, where the potential employer, the National Security Agency (NSA), had subjected me to a routine physical, an entertaining psychological quiz, the language test, and that full-scope polygraph exam; actually, two polygraphs, because I had been called back for a second examination after the first. The Alabamian examiner had warned me that I was "inconclusive" on one key question and would have to return the next day for a second try, back in the retro-futuristic Airport Square One outbuilding near the Holiday Inn where I was staying by the airport. The second round went much more smoothly (though I fell for his rookie trick of starting off with, "Which question do *you* think it was?"). I took some comfort in the gossip of the other examinees in the break room, who earnestly reassured each other that "inconclusive" was a perfectly acceptable result; O.J. Simpson, they said, by contrast, had bombed his recent polygraph exam with ninety percent DI (deception indicated) when asked whether he had murdered his ex-wife.

Why NSA? After enjoying several years of living in Los Angeles and earning a living translating and interpreting Arabic, I harbored a mounting wish for respectable, salaried work, and the government intrigued me. My beloved father had died the previous Memorial Day, and I wanted to be closer to my mother and siblings on the East Coast. As it was, I was a solitary worker who started each day in the gym and then manning my tiny office, sparring with the National Geographic Society over my next assignment, translating immigration, divorce, and citizenship papers, and over one memorably long weekend, Yemen's exhausting patent law. Those are the kind of weekends that drive people to daydream about salaried employment.

As to my time *mostly* in suburban Maryland, after the pre-employment tribal rituals at NSA near Baltimore, I headed to suburban Virginia for a day talking to federal intelligence officers; I had been translating a few thousand words of Arabic every week for them, between National Geographic fieldwork in Syria, Lebanon, and Egypt. Always open to freelance assignments, I had happily signed up for unclassified Arabic work for the Joint Publication Research Service, a nameplate for FBIS, the

Foreign Broadcast Information Service, which was the CIA's open-source intelligence collector. It monitored internet, radio, television, and print media globally, as well as "gray literature"—conference papers, in-house publications, school textbooks, and other foreign information not entirely public and yet not really secret. My friends there now fervently assured me that NSA—they expanded the acronym as "Never Say Anything"—was a dead end: a vast linoleum-floored suburban dump and that I should stay away from it. I would be much happier on their side of the Potomac, they told me, though there would be a few more hoops to jump through, they admitted, and urged me to think it over on the way home.

FBIS had assuaged one worry I had shared involving an applicant's foreign travel—I knew that they document foreign travel fastidiously in order to check with the relevant US embassies to see if you had come up on their radar while in their country. Throughout the 1990s, I had violated Clinton-era sanctions on Iraq and Lebanon by traveling there on visas issued outside my passport; this was after Madeleine Albright's State Department had denied a sanctions waiver requested by the National Geographic Society on the gaudiest letterhead I had ever seen. My concern was this would be a red flag in my background investigation, but the CIA people's reaction verged on delight that I had gotten away with it—as long as I had no close and continuing relationships arising from the travel. No, I said, except for the Christmas card that Hizballah insisted on sending to reporters. My most recent assignment, in Lebanon, involved working closely with the security and propaganda officers of that Iranian-backed terrorist group, as that group controlled southern Beirut, southern Lebanon, and the Bekaa Valley. I hated talking to their people and wanted to take a shower after every encounter with their media-savvy thugs, but none of it was illegal. "You're good," I was assured.

My in-flight reading on United 947 was *Narrow Rooms* because, spurred by several articles by one of my favorite filmmakers, John Waters, I had already read Purdy's *63: Dream Palace* and was appalled equally by Purdy's brilliance and his popularity among great writers like Paul Bowles, Edith Sitwell, Edward Albee, Tennessee Williams, Katherine Ann Porter, Gore Vidal, and many more, versus his invisibility. The year prior, I had written an article for Vanity Fair magazine that would later so animate the Saudi government against me that our asymmetric feud would still be playing out a decade later at the White House; my thinking was, might I not venture out of the Middle East and pitch the magazine a piece about Purdy? I did pitch it, and they were so receptive that my daily agenda entry a few days later read, "Call Purdy, Edward Albee, Gore Vidal." I did not know that Albee was dying.

I had recently decided to resign from contracting work for National Geographic, having tired of the Arab world. I had been sick of the hot and turbulent Middle East since leaving it in 1985. A region that once held an allure to a reporter of wealth, holy places, royalty, and war had turned stagnant and stale. Apart from the irritations of the region, there was my need to make steady money, and so I rarely said no to any assignment. Thus, the Geographic writer agreeing to fly to the Middle East for three months of fieldwork impeded the peace of mind of the guy translating a book on a deadline, who was, unfortunately, the same person.

And the Geographic's own ample resources and high editorial standards often worked against me. On assignment to research the Nile Delta, I was told in the city of Damietta, a provincial capital in the eastern Delta, that the name meant "city of cedar" in ancient Egyptian. As the article moved toward publication through the magazine's legendary fact-checkers, it was determined that cedars never grew in Damietta, and I was directed to get clarity from my informant, who speculated that it was the port city's imports of Phoenician cedar from Mount Lebanon, to build pharaohs' sarcophagi, that gave Damietta its name. (This was consistent with a quip in a history of the Lebanese civil war in which a Beirut wit told Jonathan Randall, "Every time a pharaoh died, a Lebanese made money.") By this time, I was on the follow-on assignment in Beirut, and the fact-checkers sent word of their unhappiness with the word "probably" in my explanation. But they were delighted to learn that I was only a few miles from Mount Lebanon itself—surely professors in Beirut or local cedar experts could provide certainty! I begged them to just cut the sentence from the article, but they wanted to keep it. (To my relief, there was a scholar of Phoenician culture in East Beirut who lived for questions like that and confirmed the Damiettan informant's etymology.)

I had mostly enjoyed the months in Lebanon, except for the depressing sight of portraits of Ayatollah Khomeini and other Iranian regime figures all over Beirut. But that repellent experience aside, the Geographic conceded that they had no other work for me; with their world-class Rolodex of experts, they would never offer me assignments on France, exotic diseases, cheetahs, butterflies or sunken Spanish galleons, or outer space, and so we cordially parted ways.

Purdy was more my speed. I went to Brooklyn Heights to visit the courtly, elderly novelist in his spare apartment at 236 Henry Street. I was apprehensive, given the weird and violent tenor of so many of his novels and the things other writers had said about him. "Eager to see your rape-novel!" Paul Bowles wrote to Purdy on June 1, 1967. Albee had said that what appealed to him in Purdy's work was "its wit, its eroticism ... one smells musk, is aware of breath, is brushed by the skin of the described." Fran Lebowitz told me that Purdy was "far and away, my favorite American writer," adding that "There was a real vogue for him at [Andy Warhol's] The Factory, among the two or three people who knew how to read ... he [Purdy] has an aversion to heterosexuals in conversation—very unusual of someone that age."

Over tea at Henry Street, Purdy gushed about the hideous ending of *Narrow Rooms*, calling it a "horror story." His Midwest, he said, was full of small-town horror. "It's based on a true story. These boys had a gang, and they murdered a man who had a very fine horseradish factory. He was intimate with the boys—the lawyers used that as the reason. I don't think so. He might have kissed them. But more was going on. The rest I imagined."

Of course, *Narrow Rooms* was shocking, he said. "It shocked me to write it!"

"Perchè ... Arabi?" This was Vidal's diffident first question after the obligatory one about how bad the traffic had been from Long Beach to the Westside of Los Angeles, where I had reached Sunset Boulevard at North Crescent Drive and followed an undulating path lined by palm, Ficus, and jumbo Bird of Paradise plants behind the Beverly Hills Hotel to reach the cushy pink and green Regency recesses of Bungalow 16A. Vidal knew both sides of the Mediterranean, as he conveyed in just two words, and was curious about why someone with literary siblings would learn Arabic and translate books instead of writing fiction. I had brought him a host gift of a couple of books I had written and a couple I had translated.

"Married American novelists who teach in universities and have marriage troubles possess this uncanny ability to create novels about married American novelists who teach in universities and have marriage troubles," Vidal mused as he mixed our cocktails. He was famously contemptuous of John Updike, Philip Roth, and Norman Mailer, but a certain smile, just for me, seemed to convey that he was also familiar with the work of my brothers, Alex and Paul. Then the telephone rang.

Outside, the sun was setting through the dense vegetation. The bungalows at the hotel, built around 1915 and long before air conditioning, had been designed for privacy and coolness. This meant the windows were small, and the landscaping, nearly 100 years on, was still a lavish but fastidiously controlled jungle.

"Roddy!" Vidal exclaimed, joyously rolling the R. Roddy McDowall was calling. Some of the conversation was muffled, but Vidal's decibels rose as the subject seemed to turn to reviews of his recent memoir, *Palimpsest*. Once Vidal had run out of insults for the *Advocate*'s reviewer, he seemed to be warming to a dinner invitation.

When he got off the phone, he mixed fresh cocktails and asked me about the Arab countries and Israel and what I thought about the writers there. After working through Amos Oz, A.B. Yehoshua, Emile Habibi, and Mahmoud Darwish, we eventually got around to my reason for being here, Purdy.

Of Purdy's work itself, Vidal assessed that the novelist had gone off his game, though, he conceded, he would always perjure himself in a blurb to flatter a living writer he has lost interest in. "These days, Purdy publishes first drafts. He didn't used to." He pointed to the nearby copy of his own *Palimpsest,* which he had inscribed for me *("Auguri!—Gore Vidal"). "That* is a fifth draft."

One afternoon later that week, I was filling out the CIA's laborious Personal History Statement, which required the documentation of everything from my high school and college transcripts to the start and end dates of every trip abroad since childhood, plus an essay question. I had mixed feelings about deserting LA for the soulless Beltway just as my town was suddenly becoming so interesting, and numbing paperwork has a way of encouraging mixed feelings. I was wrestling with wording my responses to questions about run-ins with the law (none) and drug use (almost none) when the phone rang.

"Theroux? ... Vidal." It was the familiar mellifluous baritone on the line, and now he was rolling the R in my surname, clearly in a chipper mood. What, pray, were my occupations this afternoon? If I was thirsty, he suggested, it would be cocktail hour by the time I reached the Westside. We could talk about Purdy some more.

My focus on the federal job search vanished at the prospect of Vidal inviting me back for more booze and gossip, especially knowing that this invitation came despite my not having flattered Vidal's famous ego. His brief comments on Purdy had enlivened the draft I was tinkering with, but I had managed to get through most of an afternoon in the luxurious bungalow without asking about himself or, for example, why he was living in a hotel in Los Angeles instead of his home on the Amalfi Coast in Italy.

It turned out he had a role in a movie. Having rented out his Hollywood house to Nicolas Cage, he had nowhere to perch for this job but this Beverly Hills bungalow along with his friend Howard, who was always napping in the next room of the two-room accommodation. We were drinking cocktails again—bourbon for him and a Bombay Sapphire martini for me.

"It's with Ethan Hawke, Jude Law, and Uma Thurman. I play an asshole named Director Josef. The movie is entitled *Figure Eight*," he said. (It would be released the following year as *Gattaca*.) His reasoning for another small acting gig—this was his third or fourth—had little to do with the appeal of the specific role. "I'm concerned literature has no future. Young people don't read books, but they watch movies."

I pointed out that no matter how much or little people read, he would at least be remembered for *Myra Breckinridge* and *Lincoln*, much as Vladimir Nabokov had conceded in an interview that despite a prolific literary and academic career, he would be a "doubly obscure" writer remembered only for *Lolita* and his translation of Pushkin's *Eugene Onegin*. Was that so bad? This elicited a genial smile as Vidal sipped his bourbon, not displeased by the comparison to Nabokov.

"At my age, I had to choose between bridge and acting, and since I don't have the memory for bridge ..." He shrugged. This led into another foray into Purdy territory, and as always, never unadjacent to Vidal territory.

"Purdy has this highly justified paranoia about why he isn't appreciated and why he's badly published. But you can't get *anything* published. In book selling, there was a great transformation when the chains married the malls. They sell something like two-thirds of all books sold. The remaining third is sold by serious book-stores. I had seven number-one bestsellers. *Lincoln* sold 250,000 books. The malls might have marginalized mid-list novelists to the lower fifteen spots out of twenty-five, but Purdy is in outer space. The fag division has been ignored for most of the century. Purdy was never let in the door except by mistake."

There was a pause, and we both noted the time. Vidal had Howard to attend to, and I had to contend with the 405 freeway. I rose and thanked him for his hospitality, citing the rush hour traffic, not only past the airport, but the South Bay Curve, for my departure.

"As you noted in your book."

I had included my nonfiction book *Translating LA* in my original gift to him. So, he had read it? Liked it?

"It was ... nice. Can you come by tomorrow? Don Bachardy will be here in the afternoon, painting my por-trait. Do you know him? You're too young to have known Christopher."

His three-syllable bad review of my book—four, counting the pause—and brisk change of subject broke new ground for me in the faint praise category.[1] But still, it was an invitation, the third one, and he had given me credit for knowing who Christopher Isherwood was, either as the author of *Berlin Stories*, as Vidal's script-writing colleague at MGM in the 1950s, or as Bachardy's late boyfriend.

I checked my pocket agenda. The following day only involved my going to Al's Fingerprinting in Long Beach so that I could document and forward my notarized fingerprints to the national security establishment and procure my college transcripts for the same audience so that I could leave this increasingly intriguing Los Angeles for the safety of a cubicle in the suburbs of Washington DC.

The following day, I got fingerprinted and headed back to Vidal's bungalow, out on the patio this time, to watch Bachardy painting him in three similar poses in a striped shirt and blazer, realistically ruddy, plump, and a little bug-eyed.

Vidal and Bachardy were deep in conversation throughout, mostly on the topic of a handsome Moroccan waiter who had intrigued them both at Roddy's dinner party. Bachardy was a highly focused portraitist, moving deftly from canvas to canvas—a Bachardy portrait session famously produced three paintings—amid all the eye-rolling and conversation. Eventually, the two of us

---

1 Only later did I realize that I had quoted him in it. From his novel *Messiah*, "Egypt one knows without visiting it, and China the same; but Los Angeles is unique in its bright horror." You'd think he'd have been pleased!

chatted as Vidal went indoors to tend to his friend. We had Morocco in common, but my stories were about mosques and cobras, and his were about Paul and Jane Bowles and Mick Jagger. He invited me to Santa Monica so he could paint me, and two weeks later, he did. As with Vidal, he painted three quick takes as I marveled at the displays all around his house of portraits of everyone from Hollywood royalty to British royalty, beside the random young plumber who had shown up to unclog a drain but stayed for three nude portraits, smiling innocently and pensively resting his head on his hand in a grand armchair with his uncircumcised manhood dominating the sightline. I signed and dated each of the three portraits of me near the upper right corner, per Bachardy's rule, and he promised to send along photographs of the pictures.

I drove back home on the freeway through the southbound 405 freeway's La Tijera bottleneck, Los Angeles Airport congestion at Century Boulevard, and the South Bay Curve, wondering if I would ever rid my life of these terrible highways. The answer—*Yes, but*—was waiting for me at home on my answering machine. A woman who identified herself only as Liza from the Recruiting Center, definitively offered to free me from the Los Angeles freeways. Her message was that the Agency had accepted the NSA's medical and polygraph and had a job for me at the GS-11 level. "Call me back."

I did call her back and, in return, was offered an EOD (Entry on Duty) date in the spring—about three months off.

In the interim, I would be granted a government-funded house-hunting trip to Washington. I promised to think it over, and she cautioned me not to dawdle.

A few days after Vidal wrapped up his scenes and left Los Angeles, my brother Paul showed up from Hawaii and wanted to attend a birthday party for a stunt actor he knew. I picked him up at his Santa Monica hotel and we headed up into the Hollywood Hills. We arrived at a home address in Beachwood Canyon at a vertiginous altitude opposite an even steeper hillside parking area and descended on a footpath into a room bright with candelabra, champagne flutes, and chattering guests, a scene familiar to anyone who has experienced the closing thirty minutes of David Lynch's *Mulholland Drive*. The stunt actor blew out the candles on his cake, and we drifted into conversations, most of which dwelled on a lunatic unknown to us named Jim Cameron and the recent wrap of a horrible movie we were warned to avoid or to see on the big screen before it sank as rapidly as its namesake.

"*Titanic*. See it fast. It will not stay afloat for the historic four hours!"

All the partygoer actors on the shoot had stories about rolling down the decks in successively various wardrobes—in tuxedoes, nightclothes, and chef uniforms. All this had taken place in a huge water tank set specially built in Rosarito Beach, in Mexico, just a four-hour drive from Hollywood. They were all so convivial and relieved that the shoot was done, and yet it had been a decent payday for a bad movie, they said.

"Do I know your work?" Paul asked a tall woman among the Titanic survivors as we all cracked up at the literary tone of his question.

"Did you see *Thelma and Louise*?" she asked. Of course, we had. "I drove off the cliff with her in the final scene." She pointed to another woman nearby. "I was Susan. She was Geena." Then what? We were truly enthralled by two women who so casually drove a speeding car off a cliff to their apparent deaths. "The car made the fall. We deployed parachutes, and we each broke an ankle because of course we did."

At that, we all toasted each other, and I could not remember when I had ever been so happy, feeling like family on this patch of Hollywood lawn overlooking the glittering Los Angeles basin below. Here were people who abounded in theatrical talent, physical courage, irony, and comedy. It was a joy to keep on toasting each other as fellow creatives, just as I was planning to suit up to join the faceless intelligence world, where the players sought clandestinity instead of fame. But even then, I sensed a kinship with the stunt actors, who worked in the shadows, whose names would never show in bright lights, but who made the mission work. As a translator, I already had a taste of that.

A day or two later, I accepted the Agency's offer, sparring a little over the start date and salary, perhaps with the subliminal hope that Liza would withdraw the offer in a fit of pique. She did not.

Around this time, my skinny young actor nephew Justin turned up in Los Angeles. Here was a family member I could torment with my dilemma. I had avoided the subject with Paul, as it might have derailed our fun in Hollywood, but Justin was close to my age (as the youngest of eight children, I am closer in age to more of my siblings' children than I am to the siblings) and a budding professional who had constantly stepped away from conventional success when it would have distracted him from the core acting and writing skills he was developing. While most moviegoers might think acting was the most glamorous line of work, one of Justin's rules was that "The writer is the architect—he writes the whole blueprint. The director is the builder—he implements the writer's vision; the actor is a leg on a table." He had quit a TV show called The District because it was bad. We, his country-mouse relations, could not imagine walking away from a primetime television role. He believed in trying for something better, and could provide an honest opinion as to whether I would be stupid or wise to leave LA.

We were sitting in a booth at the historic and comfortable Musso & Frank Grill on Hollywood Boulevard near Cherokee, fortyish me in a gray suit, white shirt and tie, and twenty-something Justin in a wife beater under a leather jacket. A New York stage actor, he was a reluctant visitor here, put up for a few weeks in Universal City to shoot scenes for *Romy and Michelle's High School Reunion*, and, it turned out, enthusing for anyone leaving despised LA, even versus his birthplace in DC, for which he had no sentimentality. His father, my oldest brother, had always been cagey about his few years at the CIA between the Army and law school, which never impressed this particular son of his.

Justin had reported for work on this movie, met his director David Mirkin, and was told, "Don't shave for a week." That left us ample time to meet.

"Damn," he said. "In New York, actors want to act, and they study the craft. In LA, they just want to be famous. You have a casting call here for a middle-aged schoolteacher, and you have two hundred nineteen-year-olds with their head shots and reels, just hoping to be discovered."

"Sir, another round for you and the young man?"

"Yes, for me and my *nephew*."

The waiter smiled and rolled his eyes a little.

Justin argued that the East Coast was better than the West, but if I needed work, I should think about New York, not Washington. His father lived in northern Virginia, and that would make Washington a little homier for me, I pointed out. No, Justin said, his dad had just accepted a job to represent his law firm in India and was getting ready to pack up his family for at least two years in New Delhi. My mother supported the move east, of course. Most of my LA friends were appalled at the notorious three initials and feared that once hired, I would not be allowed to quit. My nephew's bottom line was, follow your nose; it's all about the new.

As I was scheduling the house-hunting trip for the move to DC, a National Geographic editor called out of the blue. I had quit because I did not want any more Arab world assignments, he recalled; was Iran different enough? Mohammed Khatami had just been elected to the Iranian presidency. He was a "moderate," and the Iranian government was desperate for non-political coverage. This opening had come to the Geographic via the Iranian UN mission, where it seemed the Islamic Republic's consular officials were itching to grant an entry visa to the Geographic's chosen candidate to do fieldwork in Iran. It would be a country story—the major cities, oil regions, archaeology, borders and coasts, ecology, industries, and so on, meaning a few months in country and a good payday. I would need to contact a Mr. Sabzalian in New York, who had been involved with the Islamic Republic's liaison office in Washington DC but who was now trading on his diplomatic past to succeed as a fixer for people like me, or pathetic future versions of me.

First of all, the idea of Khatami or his ilk as moderates seemed to me a bad joke. He was not as bloodthirsty as other Iranian mullahs, but that was setting the bar preposterously low. My research into Shia affairs during the 1980s, when Khatami was Iran's Minister of Culture, had familiarized me with that ministry's propaganda, which maintained a fever pitch of anti-Semitism. It was under his supposed moderate friends, such as President Hashemi-Rafsanjani, that the regime directed the terrorist bombings of the Israeli Embassy in Buenos Aires in 1992 and of the AMIA building there two years later, killing and wounding hundreds of people; the gruesome Chain Murders against Iranian dissidents in the 1990s, and the Khobar Towers truck bombing in 1996 that killed nineteen American service members in Saudi Arabia. Most personal for me was the brazen assassination of former Prime Minister Shahpur Bakhtiar in his home in Paris. Regime agents stabbed him to death on August 6, 1991, in the same living room in suburban Sûresnes where the kindly exile had granted me an interview over tea six years earlier. Thanks to French fecklessness, his three murderers made it back to Iran to heroes' welcomes, giving me another score to settle.

I had traveled mostly unmolested in Saddam Hussein's Iraq and Mubarak's Egypt, and so I knew that countries government by dictators tended to be safer than those governed by backstabbers. Paranoid and faction-ridden governments like Iran's meant that if one faction did not like your face, they could kidnap you, and no other faction would risk defending you. That, among other reasons, had always kept Tehran in the hostage-taking business.

And then there was the CIA. Even though I was not an employee, I had been contracting for FBIS for nearly seven years. Suppose the Iranians found that out. Surely, they would know what it was? Even if they never found out that I was annually issued 1099 forms from the IRS listing the Central Intelligence Agency as a provider of miscellaneous income, supposing they interrogated or polygraphed me on the assumption that any American was probably a spy? The NSA had already taught me that I was catnip for polygraph examiners. Further, just as US embassies would assist the CIA's background checkers, any Iranian consular section would look at my travel history in the region and pulse Hizballah for details on our interactions in Lebanon. I did not want to spend the rest of my life chained to a radiator in some unpronounceable neighborhood in Tehran.

Still, I called the Recruiting Center and asked what the Agency's position would be if I requested one year's postponement of the EOD date due to travel to Iran. She got back to me promptly and said I might still be hired but that there was no guarantee. There would have to be another round of background checks and an updated medical exam.

"And a psychological exam, too," my friends joked. What American in his right mind would travel to the Islamic Republic of Iran? And really, was it much different from the Arab places I had left behind? Hmm. Certainly, every day I had spent in Lebanon offered some kind of reminder of Iran's reach there and how Hizballah had worked with the Iranians to kidnap, torture, and murder Americans. Iran itself had once had the same allure of wealth, holy places, royalty, and war that I knew from the Arab countries. Rich and glamorous LA had those things, too, thanks to its being a sort of holy land, as its movie Mecca side (the El Al billboard on Sunset Boulevard showed the Hollywood sign and the Jerusalem skyline in brilliant color, with the boast, "From one Promised Land to the Other, in 13 Hours!") and LA riots had shown.

In any event, National Geographic did successfully proceed with the Iran project—published as "Iran Behind the Veil" in 1998—which humanized Khatami's Islamic Republic just as the regime resumed its famous Chain Murders with the slaughter of political activists Dariush and Parvaneh Forouhar in Tehran later that same year and dozens more abroad. The murder of Iranian authors and dissidents inside and outside Iran proceeded lavishly in the following months and years, as the charade of Khatami's moderate presidency bought a little global cover for the regime's routine murderousness towards its opponents.

Back in LA, my fleeting, last-minute glimpses of literary and cinematic excitement during these months in California had shown glints of gold, whether pure or fool's. The job offer in Washington stood. Without the noise of celebrity or family, I could think more clearly. Was there any starker choice on earth than the one between Langley and Tehran? Still pining for water cooler banter and now intrigued by the notion of harming rather than humanizing Iran and its proxies, I decided to give the FBIS offer a year.

Founded in 1941, first known as the Foreign Broadcast Intelligence Service, FBIS predated the rest of the CIA by six years. It was part of the OSS before being taken over the US Army and then by the Agency's Directorate of Science and Technology.

Hindquarters

WITHIN THREE MONTHS, the Agency had funded a house-hunting trip to Washington, DC, and my drive east in my ancient diesel Mercedes to the apartment I had leased on California Street NW. After a two-week course at Headquarters in the basics of intelligence work, I began commuting to my job in the outer suburbs.

The FBIS building in the Virginia suburbs is filled with linguists and analysts scouring foreign newspapers, magazines, radio, television, and the internet for information of use to policymakers and other intelligence officers. It was said at the time that eighty percent of intelligence collected by the CIA was open source, such as what we did; this was a source of pride for FBIS, given that it existed in an organization whose core mission was clandestine collection. However, the outfit's pride was of the wounded variety, as FBIS was often called the CIA's "red-headed stepchild." The colloquial expression is one of debasement, referring to something that is "less than," and I heard it used about FBIS several dozen times during my first month of the job. It is true that the Service had bounced around as a foster child, if not a red-headed one, in the custody of the Directorate of Intelligence, because of its utility to analysts, and the Directorate of Science and Technology, because of its satellites. The workplace rumor was that we would eventually be spun off to the Department of Defense or made independent.

A sense of uneven self-esteem—which was sky-high elsewhere in the Agency—informed some FBIS officers' obvious bewilderment at my arrival. It generally went along these lines: "You used to travel the Middle East for National Geographic—how cool! So what on earth are you doing here?" "You went to Harvard—shouldn't you be a senator or something?"

Ironically, President Nixon had derided the CIA as "a bunch of guys out there reading newspapers." Other critics accused analysts of having poor clandestine sourcing and ignoring what was in front of their noses in the open foreign media. Indeed, every component of the CIA is a media punching bag in one way or the other. Compounding this in FBIS morale was that in a culture of recruiting spies and stealing secrets, the OSINT mission decidedly lacked sizzle, and OSINT pretty much covered what we did. (This is an acronym for Open Source Intelligence, as distinct from what is collected from human espionage; electronic or signals collection; and imagery from satellites—HUMINT, SIGINT, and IMINT, respectively.)

The fact was, as I was soon to discover, the open source mission was varied in ways I never appreciated before I joined. Most basically, FBIS helped shape the espionage mission; if we could capture information in the open media, the HUMINT collectors—the Directorate of Operations (DO), called "collector of last resort"—would not need to commit their much riskier and more expensive resources to get that information; nor would NSA. I saw more than a few eye-rolls from analysts at our coverage of state media's fastidious reports about seemingly ordinary activities of their monarch or president being seen off at his capital's airport; these trips would be for a foreign visit, domestic tour, or perhaps to take up residence at the summer capital. (I think that was when I heard my first "Seriously?") Analysts were not the customers for this kind of information. It was for the intelligence community that reliable details of VIP travel were vital.

We also monitored covert actions, which is jargon for reading the online or hardcopy media that global clandestine services owned or in which they planted stories to influence their adversaries. For Arabic linguists, this was a busy line of business, given the number of rogue regimes and terrorist groups originating in the Middle East and who were active globally. We were busy detecting the hand of foreign intelligence services and other actors, diligent when it came to the influence line of work. We had to be sure that our analysts and other consumers did not use such deliberately unreliable information as sources in their analysis.

While open source information is easy to collect—no need to set up covert asset meetings or task satellites like our big-budget, high-morale colleagues—only novices among our DI and DO colleagues thought what we pulled in was unclassified. At any given time, tons of secret information are sloshing around in the open media—planted, leaked, or compromised for any number of reasons and in every language under the sun.

Propaganda isn't generally hard to spot, but it was important for us to keep in mind how subtle, well-crafted influence ops by bad actors could be. Sifting through the foreign media for leaks was the most rewarding open-source work of all. We had to be on the lookout for how politicians, legislators, and journalists in some countries used leaks to conduct complicated feuds. For example, senior Muslim religious clerics and mosque preachers provided us with impressive insights once they started up their websites; on these, they derided not only "Crusaders," Jews, and infidels but each other as well in ways that revealed how they perceived their government's marching orders. One huge leak of clandestine information on the Lebanese terrorist group Hizballah, by a whistleblower or terror sympathizer (or both), was sent to the media from a government and gave important information about this particular government. All of the information was valid and about half of it we already knew. But we did not know the other half as it had apparently been withheld from us. Once US analysts with access to relevant classified information dissected the information, it yielded insights from the counterterrorism and counterintelligence perspectives. It was clear to us that Hizballah and both other adversaries as well as partners of ours would read the story and also gain some level of insight, giving us—the Agency, NSA, our military, and all our national security partners—another level of more careful behaviors to stay on top of. All of this resulted from a page of public newsprint. (I have to wonder, does that Nixon crack still bug me?)

Of course, we read, translated, and analyzed foreign media for more conventional reasons, for example, having to do with military, industrial, and economic data. However, even seemingly unrelated information could be surprisingly subtle and revealing; one of my colleagues was able to assess the Iraqi order of battle from public coverage of matches played by the various military units' soccer teams around the country. We passed a photograph from a Baghdad newspaper of Saddam Hussein visiting the hospital room of his ailing vice president, Izzat Ibrahim al-Duri, to the Directorate of Intelligence (DI)—important because even a simple photo like this might have publicly displayed clues. At times photos of this sort complemented findings from clandestine collections on senior leaders' health, always of interest to policymakers. Another example was our scrutiny of the televised body language of ailing foreign leaders and those around them, which would help determine in some cases that one was losing his sight or in which ear another leader was deaf.

Diplomatic cables from the US embassies in the Persian Gulf avidly reported on the local media and tended to spin positive, for example, reporting glowingly on reports of a Saudi-Iranian thaw (an elusive and often illusory target under the artful and murderous Khatami). FBIS did some definitive work on the same media reporting, revealing it to be the work of two assiduous Iranian diplomats who chose the same receptive journalists with whom they shared wishful thinking, probably to soften up Arab readers to the idea that a thaw was a good thing, and quickly rerun by other media who were not picky about their sub-sourcing.

After our policymakers visited a foreign country, they would have us provide roundups of the local media coverage of their time there. Since I covered mostly the Arabian Peninsula and Iraq, I was always giving them bad or outright offensive news. Secretary of State Madeline Albright insisted on seeing editorial cartoons of her—which, in Saddam's Iraq, could have graced the pages of Germany's Nazi publication, *Der Stürmer*—but she was a good sport about it. Once, in the late 1990s, we detected a sign of shift in the Saudi editorial line towards Saddam in a cartoon portraying a nude patient sitting on an examining table—his head was a globe of the earth labeled THE ARAB WORLD—and instead where the patient's buttocks should have been was Saddam's face. The doctor was saying to him, "You won't regain your health until that malignancy is removed." We disseminated this with a brief and lightly classified commentary on the level of control Riyadh kept over the portrayal of Arab leaders. The White House feedback was positive, and it probably gave Secretary Albright a smile.

My first taste of liaison work involved an assignment to a Spanish-speaking country for several months. Our office there was coordinating with the host country service to collect against Arabic-speaking terrorist targets and needed a language specialist. In preparation, I took a quick course in survival Spanish. I arrived in the country eager to impress local Agency leadership with my Spanish as a quick study. The deputy station chief welcomed me into an office arrayed with awards and mementoes from past work with liaison services all over the world. The collection included some challenge coins, diploma-like citations, inscribed Lucite obelisks, and grand medallions laid in velvet cases like jewelry, along with the prevalent theme— shiny bladed weapons mounted on wooden plaques.

"Hablas español?" he asked, drawing a prompt *"Francamente, yo hablo español limitado"* from me, and we continued for a few minutes in an increasingly wobbly conversation. "Fantastic!" was his reaction, much to my

surprise. Surely, I modestly responded, my Spanish was not fantastic? "No, your Spanish sucks," he answered with a grin. "That's fantastic because you'll spend half your time here working at the host service headquarters. They don't speak English there, and we were concerned that if your Spanish was good, they'd be eliciting stuff from you. But we're safe."

My job was to listen to and analyze dozens of hours of telephone conversations in Arabic. The mostly Levantine dialects in use were easy to understand. The tough part was the speakers' "comsec," or communications security. They never discussed their movements. Fortunately, in the early days of cellphones, one per family was common, and while a narcotrafficker who had terrorist friends might be too careful to talk on the phone about his travel plans, his teenage daughters, mixing Arabic and Spanish, were blessedly innocent of counterintelligence concerns. Between breathless exchanges about which female classmate was a *bruja* or a *cerda*, or which boy was *guapo*, girls freely expressed regret that she would lose access to the phone when *Papi* took it with him Tuesday on his trip to Beirut, Dubai, and *la isla Kish*, wherever that was!

Despite their reticence when it came to travel plans, our targets were surprisingly loose-lipped about trafficking weapons and cocaine, along with one other commodity for which I assessed they used a special cover term, *La Sirenita*. Busily taking expert notes as I listened to their rapid Arabic mingled with English and Spanish, I planned to cover myself with analytic glory by deciphering these tantalizing references. A few days later, a conversation with a station colleague revealed, to my chagrin, that VHS videocassettes of Disney's *The Little Mermaid* were a hot smuggling commodity.

That assignment was also my introduction to compartmentation—the walling-off of some programs from anyone who did not require "must-know" access to the information, distinct from the "need to know" that came with a routine Top Secret clearance. My boss loaned me to a sensitive collection site—not declared to the host country, I recall—which required cables to NSA, and my being granted a special clearance before I could even learn the work location. I was cautioned not to discuss, even in the office, what the work there was like. When it was time to go home to the US, a cable went to Headquarters praising my work, enumerating the intelligence reports we had disseminated and the extent of operational support provided. The special site gave me even more enthusiastic feedback in person, but my FBIS bosses back home were not cleared to hear it. And so, there was a mere sentence added to the cable mentioning my "support to the signals mission."

In time, the language work I was doing, having returned home, began to feel ancillary to me. While we were helping enable a mission, we were not out in front. Several months of attending other people's meetings piqued my growing interest in all source analysis. Whereas my focus was mostly on media in the vernacular, all source DI analysts read media plus diplomatic cables, HUMINT and SIGINT reporting, and imagery. They talked to our foreign liaison partners, and wrote analytic assessments based on everything the Intelligence Community (IC) had seen.

There were four analytic disciplines: political, economic, military, and leadership. As a linguist, I had analytic customers in the DI who directed and followed my work, including a new hire, David Priess, who would later write a book about the DI, Bruce Riedel, who would help me get a job at the White House, and John Kiriakou, who had a distinctly different outcome. He was an Iraq analyst who was eventually convicted for leaking the identity of covert operatives, after which he joined a Russian television station having served his prison term here. Overall, these were some of the most erudite, congenial, and witty people I had ever met. In late December, they held a hilariously entertaining holiday event in which various analytic offices put on hilarious skits—these were unclassified if held in a restaurant's reserved spaces, but if held inside Headquarters they could mock their managers at the top-secret level. The only downside I experienced with this group was the long hours they worked. I admit that I had a soft spot for the affable Kiriakou. He spoke Arabic well and was one of the rare analysts who was willing to venture out to our FBIS building, but I did recall how, fifteen years before Kiriakou's conviction, a prescient leadership analyst commented to me out of the blue that "I wouldn't trust Kiriakou farther than I could throw him." Finally, my water cooler daydream was about to be realized.

"We tell the truth to power" was the mantra often heard around the DI. It was not unlike what the "red-headed stepchild" was to FBIS—the contrast illustrates the widely different self-image—and it got old just as fast.[2] Another ubiquitous phrase was "The First Customer," referring to the President, as the DI's most prestigious product was the Presidential Daily Brief or PDB. In the main, the analytic items in the PDB were deep and consequential. Experts, coordinating with a dozen components within the building, were challenged to write a complex and well-sourced story that would be worthy of a President's attention and often would compel a decision. All of this had to be finalized *on a single page.*

"Tradecraft" is a word unique to the intelligence world, mostly used in the DO. It means operational savvy in spotting, assessing, developing, recruiting, and handling a foreigner or network of foreign agents with access to vital clandestine information. "DI tradecraft," drilled into CIA analysts throughout their careers, is as exacting but refers to the division's writing. It means producing analytic writing that is clear and concise, expert, well-sourced, stripped of bias and emotion, stating a bottom

---

[2] I first became aware of the term in the doubly-obnoxious contact of Rashid Khalidi's "Edward Said and the American Public Sphere: Speaking Truth to Power,"a talk delivered in New York in 1996.

line made impervious to any skepticism, counterargument, or devil's advocacy; it incorporates all the DO's work and thus is of higher value. Some of our instructors liked to cite a Russian saying from the KGB days: "A spy thinks like the devil and writes like an angel." This was totally applicable to the preparation of the PDB. Its editors were notoriously harsh; PDB authors going home following a late-night sparring with the editors, often headed back into Headquarters at five o'clock the next morning. Their purpose was to pre-brief the PDB briefers as they prepared to present the analysis to the President and his inner circle and answer all follow-up questions relating to the strength of the sourcing, implications, challenges to their reasoning, and so on. The cost to family life for frequent PDB authors led them to display family photos at their workstations with a husband's, wife's, or sometimes a baby's picture with the mutinous label "FIRST CUSTOMER."

In time, I joined the Arabian Peninsula group as a political analyst in what was then called DI/NESAF, thankfully an acronym describing the Near East, South Asia, and Africa Office. The morning meeting there consisted of the group managers and all of the analysts, with one or two collection management officers from the DO, who were the main link to HUMINT collectors. We might have guest analysts sitting in from FBIS or from a functional office such as CIC (the Counterintelligence Center), the Counternarcotics Center, or even an NSA representative, depending on what looked interesting in the overnight reporting—the "traffic"—we had read. If the raw reporting met threshold, we would decide whether it was urgent enough for a PDB or for a less sensitive product, which Congress and the rest of the IC would read. At the same time, the analysts had their own long-form, in-depth reports they were working on. Another line of work was briefings, and we were always in and out of training.

Beyond all that, the basic writing lessons focused on the future rather than the past, and being chary of expressing certainty. Our adversaries were crafty, and most were proficient at D & D, which is to say, denial and deception. For example, if a satellite found what looked like tank tracks in a given location, they might be tank tracks, or they might be a deceptive effort to try to look like tank tracks. With that in mind, we would refer to them as being "consistent with tank tracks." That language would then be coordinated with the military analysts, who might be able to specify the type of tank.

CIA analysis was non-prescriptive, and as not being a policy agency, our job was only to describe and analyze things. In fact, the CIA had been established on the Virginia side of the Potomac specifically to distance itself from the DC policy world. Our counterparts back at the cabinet departments near the White House, at Treasury and State, always concluded their reports with prescriptions: for example, country X must rationalize its economy, float its currency, and ease up on dissidents. We, on the other hand, just delivered the problems we discerned with the awkwardness of being the bad-news people without solutions, though we could lay out options and comment on the first-, second- and third-order implications of potential policy actions.

This led to a crisis between the Clinton White House and the CIA around the time I joined the DI, many time zones away from the Arabian Peninsula. The scenario involved a Western hemisphere leader who had been ousted from power as president in a coup, and US policy was to reinstate him. The CIA analytic line was that the leader was unstable and that his reinstatement would lead to a long list of bad outcomes. The White House continued to ask its questions based on the assumption that he would be returned to power. Somehow, the DI had failed to appreciate that the White House had concluded this as a firm decision and, therefore, had not made it part of DI analysis. Unable to prescribe policy and all too addicted to being right, CIA just kept on repeating their bad news, which was now useless and grated on an administration that had already made up its mind. This priggishness resulted in losing the audience, which in this case was the President. Not only did Bill Clinton stop taking his morning PDB briefing, he directed National Security Advisor Sandy Berger and White House Chief of Staff John Podesta to take it on his behalf. Berger was a leaker and creep of epic proportions, and of course, this became an intelligence failure case study.

In hindsight (I hate hindsight), the disconnect from the policy world of the executive branch we served was only part of the problem. Related was the workplace cult of analysts telling the truth (a self-aggrandizing view of their analysis) to (increasingly skeptical) power. In the hard world of espionage, language officers might be stepchildren, but the analyst was, to paraphrase Gore Vidal, the brother-in-law. These alien integers are prized for their expertise but, until the September 2001 attacks broke down the bureaucratic stovepipes and turned many of us into targeters, the analysts' return address was the ivory tower. (The emerging targeting discipline developed analysts into creators of opportunities in the espionage realm, a long-needed hybrid of expert/operator.) The image of the analyst as a lone gunslinger in the badlands of crass ops officers lives on in many Agency memoirs, most ludicrously in former CIA Director John Brennan's memoir, *Undaunted*. (The title neatly sums up the whole self-regarding three hundred pages.)

Closer to home was the mystery surrounding Khobar Towers. This was the terrorist attack against US military personnel in Saudi Arabia's Eastern Province on June 25, 1996. It had been carried out by Lebanese Hizballah and a number of Saudi Arabian Shia Muslims belonging to Hizballah al-Hijaz, and trained in the Syrian- and Hizballah-controlled Bekaa Valley. The truck bomb explosion used in the attack was so loud it was heard on the nearby island of Bahrain. It was clearly Iranian-sponsored, as not only was Hizballah an Iranian creation, but Ruhollah Khomeini refused to use the name Saudi Arabia, referring to that country as Hejaz, the province where the holy cities of Mecca and Medina were located. All of this was known. The main two terrorists had fled to Iran and were among the FBI's 10 Most Wanted. But for some reason, this was a "compartmented"—limited access—issue, with only two of our analysts "read into the program." I wondered—what was the mystery? What was I missing? Of course, the Iranians had directed the attack, using their assets in the Syrian Baath regime of Hafez al-Assad and Lebanese Hizballah. Of course, the Saudis had idiotically cleaned up the crime scene, depriving us of vital forensic evidence. One of the Saudi operatives, Jaafar Shweikhat, idiotically fled to Syria for protection, where the double-dealing Syrian regime arrested him and—foreseeing a Saudi extradition request—promptly reported his suicide in prison.

I eventually made my way onto the bigot list[3] of this compartment, meaning someone was read out so that I could be read in. I was still confused. I perceived no great revelation. I reached the unclassified assumption that Iran had committed a blatant act of war against the United States, and we had them dead to rights. But since Washington had chosen not to retaliate, in spite of the high degree of Iranian culpability, it had to be hidden. A

---

[3] A British intelligence term of contested origin, meaning the roster of specially cleared officers with access to an exceptionally sensitive program. It may have been an operation codeword during Operation Overlord in World War II.

few years later, the issue was de-compartmented, bringing it down to the mere Top Secret level. There was no great secret or mystery, except for those like me wondering, as I would keep wondering for the next two dozen years, why the US government found it so hard to respond to Iranian acts of war.

Khobar Towers had been a largely historic issue, which we stayed on top of given the fugitives' presence in Iran and its being part of the ups and downs of the Saudi-Iranian relationship. Real-time terrorism came into my career on October 12, 2000. I showed up at work early and sleepy. After punching in my PIN, turning the combination of the Unican, recording my initials and the time and date, and disarming the vault (when you are the first to show up at work at CIA, you start the day feeling like a safecracker) it was amid the simultaneous ringing of almost every telephone in the vault. Our boss was not coming in that day, so assuming something horrible had just happened, I went into his office. I figured if there was panic in the building, I might as well talk to the highest-ranking of my panicky masters.

It was the Director's office, known to us as the Seventh Floor. I learned that an apparent suicide attack in Aden Harbor against the USS Cole had killed more than a dozen service members, and NESAF and CTC (Counterterrorism Center) officers were requested to provide a full briefing in the Director's conference room at ten AM. This was my first crisis, a sickening one and overwhelming. Americans had been murdered in a country that had long been a terrorist safe haven; the pressure now was to learn everything about it in two hours and provide a full briefing to the CIA director. The next colleague through the door was Andy, who paused at the sight of me sitting at our boss's desk with twenty phones still ringing. I wonder which of these he found more worrying.

We logged on and feverishly read all the situation reports from the US Embassy in Sanaa, Yemen, answered some of the phones, and called our counterparts at State and Defense Departments. Andy was my senior in pay grade, but the southern Peninsula was more my area of expertise, so he deferred to me to lead the briefing; even our CTC colleague would defer to us. On top of most of the reporting, but still feeling underprepared, we left at a few minutes to ten to walk the length of the building and up to the seventh floor. About halfway there, Andy halted and put his hand on my arm.

"Wait a minute," he said. "This is all wrong. We're all set to give them a great update, but these people run the CIA. They know all that already. No question they've already talked to the ambassador in Sanaa and the secretary of defense and CIA people in the field."

With about three minutes to go, we feverishly replayed what to say. We speculated that we would be asked what our production plans were—surely a PDB to run in the morning. Aden Harbor was a crime scene—the FBI was probably already getting a plane ready to move a hundred special agents in with guns drawn. We would be asked for an assessment of how that would be received based on what we knew of the Yemeni intelligence and law enforcement services. We would be asked what risks that would entail—what spy services had penetrated the Yemeni services, risking the information we would undoubtedly share with them in a joint counterterrorism investigation. Why were we such idiots as not to have called a counterintelligence (CI) analyst to join us? Lastly, but most urgently, our Director, George Tenet, would have to talk to President Clinton, and either or both of them would be telephoning President Salih of Yemen later today. We would have to provide background material for that.

That was a lesson I should have remembered from the initial two-week training course: Analysts are not journalists, professors, or detectives, focused on the news, the past, or evidence, but on the future.

The briefing went reasonably well. In retrospect, after the years I would spend elsewhere at State, Defense, and other cabinet agencies, the lack of hierarchy at CIA was striking. Andy and I were, respectively, GS-13 and GS-12 analysts, facing almost a dozen of the CIA's most senior officers. They were good listeners, called us by our first names after brief introductions, and included us in their deliberations about what to do next.

The next weeks and months were busy and helped my reputation. In a group that looked at highly consequential issues like Persian Gulf energy, and leadership and military issues of great interest to policymakers, my turf was the southern part of the Peninsula. Here, disgruntled Yemeni tribes would strap explosives on a donkey and let it walk towards a police checkpoint, where it would be detonated remotely. "Peter is our front line of defense against donkey bombs" was a typical gibe.

The years 2000 and 2001 were a rough ride. The turbulence originated chiefly from the Palestinian territories, where the peace process was a smoking hole thanks to the Second Intifada. Saudi Arabia and the little "Gulfies"—the Gulf Cooperation Council states—were panicking. This was not because of the Israeli and Palestinian body count but because their populations were getting restive, whipped up by the Qatari station al-Jazeera. Both Saddam Hussein of Iraq and terrorist groups such as al-Qa'ida were thought to be gaining in popularity thanks to the television images of violence in the territories and within Israel. Unsure as to whether inflammatory mosque sermons would placate or infuriate their citizens, the Saudi royals gave free rein to imams to curse infidels in the most violent terms.

Late one evening, when my neighborhood friends and I were enjoying a gin-irrigated Bad Movie Night (we had selected 2001's abominable *Glitter* with Mariah Carey and Max Beesley), my boss phoned and asked me to go into the office immediately. He needed someone to monitor events overnight because Israeli Defense Forces had rolled into Ramallah and surrounded the Muqata'ah, the compound where Yasser Arafat was holed up. Apparently, those at the top level of the US government were hearing shrieks of outrage either from Arab leaders, our ambassadors in their countries, or both. My boss would not go into detail over an open line.

I dutifully went into the building and blearily went through the steps to open the vault. Panic and outrage were indeed pouring in from the region. Although Arafat would survive, it was not without the resentment of his fellow PLO leaders, as he hogged the remote AC and heat control in his sleeping bag while the rest of them sweltered. (One later said this summed up the way he governed.) I felt more than positive that, were it not for restive populations and regime preservation, the Arab leaders would have been happy to see Arafat vaporized by Israeli artillery. He and Abu Nidal had threatened and extorted them for decades. The damage to US popularity was looking severe, and the Saudis sent Secretary of State Colin Powell a lengthy memo, much of it in all capitals, outlining their dire sense of the direction the region's security was taking.

Later, during intense peace negotiations, there seemed to be the possibility of a real breakthrough for a two-state solution for the Israelis and the Palestinians. There was a sticking point, however, and that was Jerusalem. Neither Israel nor the US wanted it divided, and American diplomats, policymakers, and intelligence analysts were racking their brains trying to come up with a formula that would satisfy all the parties. There were a number of options; one was a de facto administrative division with no physical barrier, another involved internationalizing the city, something else called "Sovereignty unto God," and still more. Most of these involved declaring Jerusalem the joint capital of both Israel and Palestine, with the Arab village of Abu Dis, about one mile east of the Old City, the site of the Palestinian government.

You could solve nearly every inch of Jerusalem's surface area until you got to the Temple Mount. It was there that the triumphalist Caliph Omar had built al-Aqsa Mosque to signal to the Jews and the world that there was a new faith in town. The Israelis suggested something like joint horizontal sovereignty, with Israel having control over the surface buildings and human movements while Palestine would technically have sovereignty of the land beneath. That was not going to work, as neither side would settle for anything less than total control over its holy places.

Before the process inevitably broke down, the time came for the US to provide a detailed briefing on the issue to the Saudi leadership. As the custodians of Mecca and Medina, Saudi buy-in was crucial for a solution on Jerusalem. The maps and imagery of Jerusalem were exemplars of fastidious labeling, with scale scrupulously indicated. To the surprise of the senior US officials doing the presentation, the Saudi response was confusion, followed by consternation and something like hilarity.

These had nothing to do with the merits of the US or Israeli proposals regarding this city, which was at the heart of the Arab and Islamic passion regarding the Palestinian issue: This was Jerusalem. Here was the Old City inside its walls—*this* was Jerusalem? the Saudis asked. This? It was so tiny! Was this a joke? The most senior Saudi royal present was fairly gasping with contempt over the holy city his country's thousands of mosque preachers were screeching about every week. He looked at the map and shook his head in disbelief. "I have palaces ten times that size," he snorted.

Dr. Condi Rice hired me to be her Director of Persian Gulf Affairs
despite the obstreperous lobbying of some Gulf diplomats.

The Lights Are Much Brighter There

I SPENT THE EARLY hours of September 11, 2001, on a red-eye flight from San Francisco to Washington, DC. I was sleepily reading *Uncle Tom's Cabin* as part of a vow to finally read all the classics I had never read, or had only in *Classics Illustrated* versions as boy. Like every other reader, I was struck by how the legendary novel that started as a sentimental potboiler got so much better and darker as it progressed to the brilliant but hideous end, when we learn the fate of the saintly Tom.

The money, of which Chloe was so proud, was still lying on the table.

"Thar," said she, gathering it up, and holding it, with a trembling hand, to her mistress, "don't never want to see

nor hear on't again. Jist as I knew 'twould be—sold, and murdered on dem ar' old plantations!"

I finished the book at about five AM as the plane approached Dulles Airport. Sliding the paperback into the seat back pocket in front of me, I sighed, thinking that at least horrible things like that don't happen anymore.

No one needs my account of that sickening day. In the days following, CIA created the Office of Terrorism Analysis (OTA). CTC, founded in the old days to study Basque terrorists, the IRA, and Palestinians who were hijacking planes, had lacked a strong analytic cadre until this point, and every DI office had to provide its quota of analysts to lash up with the DO to work on the al-Qa'ida target in OTA. A few days after the attacks, my boss and I were sent to the Liaison Suite a few floors below Tenet's office to pre-brief two foreign visitors before their meeting with the director. These were ambitious and highly trusted national security officers, usually somewhere between silky and ebullient in their exchanges with us, but with the emergence of the fact that their countries' intelligence services were about to come under the harshest of scrutiny, the two sat there ashen and mostly silent as my boss and a CT officers laid out for them what would be under discussion upstairs.

My boss turned down my offer to go over to OTA, as NESAF had to keep up its own staffing strength to partner with the new office. Eventually, the al-Qa'ida leadership would be crushed, but someone had to help the US administration worry about the right things in the meantime.

Around this time, one project of mine helped me further transition from an open source (OSINT) officer to an analyst. I had found online a hundred-page document entitled *al-Tibyan fi Kufr man A'iyan al-Amrikan,* or The Demonstration of the Unbelief of Those Who Help the Americans, by a radical Saudi cleric, the rhyming title being the fanatics' subtle homage to medieval Arabic literature. It was an unhinged, albeit fastidiously sourced and footnoted screed damning every Muslim leader who had ever cooperated with infidels, polytheists, or Jews—an implicit warning to the Saudi government not to work with the US. It was endorsed by a slew of Saudi clerics, signed by its author, Nasir bin Hamad al-Fahd, in Riyadh, and dated in the Islamic calendar 10 Shaaban, 1422, or October 27, 2001. It was hard to say which was more appalling—the content, the brazenness of the authors challenging the Saudi government, or the white heat in which the huge document had been written in the short weeks since the al-Qa'ida attacks.

FBIS linguists were working nearly around the clock to support CT efforts and had no time even to look at this document, let alone translate or discuss it. Based on my arguments, my boss and colleagues agreed it might be significant but pointed out that the White House probably did not care what Peter thought was a fascinating read.

So, we held a "murder board" meeting to gauge the threshold for caring about al-Fahd's work. What was its significance? I pointed out that the Saudi clerical establishment, or *ulama,* virtually co-governed the country as they controlled the mosques, schools, universities, and some of the media. The ulama had religious attachés in Saudi embassies around the world to enforce their dogmas and make sure the diplomats prayed five times a day. If they felt emboldened enough to publish this thing openly, they must have scented weakness in Riyadh's resolve, and let's not underestimate their ability to discern vulnerability. What were the second- and third-order implications? Saudi Arabians would read this thing—which had drawn no government response thus far—and find it consistent with everything they had been taught. They would look for their ruling family not to get involved in a war on the American side.

My DI sparring partners doubted Riyadh cared what its citizens thought. And—what made this presidential? What was the news that the White House could use here? Was there any? At the end of an hour, it was agreed that we would write a "warning piece" to sensitize the administration to the fact that, as we asked the Saudis to do more and more—hunt down al-Qa'ida members and donors, share intelligence, tell their crazier mosque imams to shut up, direct state-controlled media to support or at least not propagandize against the war effort—they had a strong domestic constituency that supported terrorism and which they had to placate somehow. We did this that day in half a page, which was then further reduced to a text box in someone else's broader analytic assessment on domestic political headwinds facing our allies. (I was used to being cut down to size like this at the Geographic, where a few hundred words of the story were routinely sacrificed when Cartography, Art, or Photography had a brighter idea for page space.)

When Tenet directed the formation of a tiger team to produce a targeting study on Osama bin Laden, I was the "stuckee" from our group. A group of about a dozen mostly senior CIA officers were offered access to every compartment, RH (restricted handling) channel of reporting, and special access program to accomplish this goal. We were also empowered to summon anyone we wanted to debrief. We talked to former DDI (deputy director for Intelligence) Winston Wiley, as well as the FBI agent who tackled CIA shooter Mir Aimal Kasi somewhere in southern Asia, a multi-tour station chief who had made inroads with members of the Bin Laden family, and Alec Station boss Mike Scheuer, among many others.

Bin Laden emerged as a canny reader of Saudi governmental behavior who had also developed a fair sense of what the US government had arrayed against him. He was a physical coward whose combat experience and courage were highly overrated; like Yasser Arafat, he had won most of his battles at a microphone. In al-Qa'ida propaganda, one of his epic moments was eluding US troops at the battle of Tora Bora. Most of our study was as highly classified as the source material we had access to, but you did not have to be an analyst of any kind to see that, in a holy war where valor and martyrdom were sacred objectives, he had simply run away to save his skin.

I doubted our work would make much of a difference.

As the years wore on, the chief HVT-1 (high-value target-1) effort became so compartmented that, for most of us, it disappeared until he was located and killed. I knew the woman (portrayed as Maya in the movie *Zero Dark Thirty*) whose targeting prowess would lead special forces to Bin Laden. One of a very small team of targeters—"Maya" was a composite—she was an unusual woman with a temper, and despite her relative youth, people were frightened by her. I thought our tiger team was too senior, too male, and well-rested to figure out Bin Laden, and that it would take a terrorist to catch a terrorist, and I was right.

By this point, I had been promoted twice and was to be rewarded with a policy rotation. I did not want one, having no desire to go "Downtown," as the capital of the United States is known at CIA headquarters (being a global intelligence service, we called our building, located in suburban McLean, "Washington"). I wanted to be sent up to NSA on rotation to improve my Arabic and learn the signals intelligence mission. No, I was told, DI analysts serve the policymaker and had to learn to do policy work to see how intelligence helped them do the job—whether or not our work was as timely and relevant as it needed to be. I was to serve for one year as the Arabian Peninsula officer at the State Department's Policy Planning Staff under Richard Haass. This was seen as a plum assignment that would get me out of the building for some perspective, and since I lived in the District, not least of it was that I could now commute by bicycle.

Before letting me go, my boss remarked that these

good things were happening to me despite my intelligence failure. He gave me a Look. I didn't get it. He was serious, and he had a point: Unlike Maya, I had been unable to think like a terrorist. This was in a branch meeting, so he had an eager audience watching him cut me down to size.

"You had your eyes on the region for three years. The terrorists moved from donkey bombs to car bombs. Then, from car bombs to truck bombs against our embassies in Nairobi and Dar al-Salaam in 1998. Next, a boat bomb against the USS Cole in 2000. Look at the trajectory. Al-Qa'ida went from crawling to walking to running. They weaponized one mode of transportation after the other, taking only a year or two for each step: car, truck, boat, plane. After the Cole, smart analysts should have noticed this and wondered how terrorists might weaponize a plane. A good murder board on that might have led to analysis resulting in stronger cockpit doors on commercial jets."

A response was forming on my tongue: *Thanks, Hal, you've had a year and a half of hindsight to come up with your zinger—where was this wondrous intellect of yours in early 2001?* But I let it go. As Lynda Obst observes, "Personal humiliation and career-dashing confrontations are endemic, impersonal, and constant. This is the flip side of ambition: debilitating exhaustion and the constant threat of defeat." And so I said nothing.

He shrugged. "Never mind, you won't have to think this hard-working for Haass."

Everywhere an Oink Oink

H E WAS RIGHT. I did not have to work hard at the State Department except to try to figure out the culture. Unlike the one at CIA, State was hierarchical and turfy. People there used titles and sharp elbows. The regional bureaus considered the overarching, global-oriented Policy Planning Staff to be a nuisance and militantly declined to share its cables with us before they were released. Because our office spaces were not SCIFs (sensitive compartmented information facilities), we had to lock up classified materials in safes overnight and could only view top secret documents on a read-and-return basis when an officer from State's Bureau of

Intelligence and Research (INR) came around pushing a little trolley of intelligence reports with cover sheets in manila envelopes. At CIA, by contrast, you could leave Top Secret material all over the desk, walls, and floor of your vault.

It dawned on me that the hierarchy at State gave even desk officers a sense of importance, given their daily exposure to foreign diplomats. Their CIA counterparts, on the other hand, were confined to cubicles in Langley (even though we never called it that) and had no such pretensions. In my first week at State, I witnessed a remarkable performance by the Kuwait-Bahrain desk officer, a twenty-year-old-something woman, when a visiting ambassador paid a pro forma compliment to a painting behind the officer's desk. This was a throwaway compliment on his part to ease the way into some rapport-building and then into the business at hand: this newly-arrived ambassador's having been frozen out of all the political contacts he should have had. His predecessor, had, for some reason, taken his Rolodex with him when he departed.

"Yes, my dad loves the abstract, but he loves color and is really into Motherwell. He got me into abstract expressionism before I was in middle school."

Our Gulf ambassador nodded politely at this, waiting for the opening to Iran, Saudi Arabia, the Palestinians, or energy issues, which were his talking points, along with some help about which US officials he needed to engage.

"My sister was at Julliard, which was fine, but when I

went to BU, my parents got way more into it, and all my walls were like riots of color."

As the Gulf ambassador's eyes glazed over (along with mine), attempting to understand State Department culture.

We very occasionally met with Colin Powell and his deputy, Richard Armitage. There was a baseline for the effectiveness of the staff: The head of Policy Planning had to have the ear of the Secretary of State, and the Secretary of State had to have the ear of the President. In 2002, President Bush did not listen to Secretary Powell, and Powell did not listen to Haass.

One upside to the job was the frequency of working-level White House meetings and State's being within walking distance from there. A feature of almost every meeting was the daylight between the NSC (National Security Council), who were administration officials whose priority was to implement the President's foreign policy, and career State officers who had to manage relationships with foreign governments and their embassies here before, during, and after any administration. A frequent question about Saudi Arabia was whether Riyadh had "got it" yet on terrorism. The NSC thought not, while State tended to plead Riyadh's case. Mosque sermons in Saudi Arabia were still bloodcurdling, and the Saudis were still supplying Muslim chaplains in US prisons with materials that incited intolerance against Jews and Christians. In these policy meetings where I nominally represented State, I usually sided with the NSC.

One day I got a call from Elliott Abrams, the NSC's Senior Director for Near East and North African Affairs. "I'd like you to come over to discuss staffing decisions at the White House." Happy to provide input to anyone in the French Empire grandeur of the Eisenhower Executive Office Building, away from the linoleum and relative idleness of State, I accepted.

Elliott's careful language was a job offer for me to take over the position of Director of Persian Gulf Affairs, about to be vacated by another CIA analyst, Phil Mudd. This was a flattering offer, but I told him that the Agency had an agreement with State that I would staff my position for a year, and I did not have the authority to do otherwise.

"Haass is going to leave State to run the Council on Foreign Relations, and he has a good reputation for looking after his people. He'll be fine with it. You'll have to interview with Condi Rice and her deputy, Steve Hadley. If that goes right and the President wants you here, your boss at CIA can't say no. At best, the Agency can decide at which level they will lose the argument."

With no sure indication that the White House job would truly be mine, I could not conceal my delight at it even being a possibility. Even my family members, who disliked the Bush administration out of concern that the war in Iraq would come—which it did within weeks— were excited at the thought.

My family were not the only ones to get early word of the job opportunity.

"Rihab was here yesterday, and your name was taken in vain," Deborah Jones told me pleasantly later that week. Deborah was Director of the Office of Arabian Peninsula Affairs and Iran, and I knew her personally from my visits to the Near East Bureau at State. (She would later serve as ambassador to Kuwait and Libya.) Rihab Massoud was the oleaginous number two in the Saudi Embassy, a close associate of Ambassador Bandar bin Sultan and often his messenger. "The Saudis are not happy at the idea of your being on the NSC."

The Saudis were not happy with me at all. On top of having written about their kingdom in a book, I had translated three books by one of their prominent dissidents—Munif—and published an article in Vanity Fair critical of Bandar himself. I had further endeared myself to them by writing commentaries about their failure to take seriously the man known in the mid-1990s merely as "terrorist financier Osama Bin Laden," and during visits to Beirut and Damascus, I befriended some of their exiled Shia Muslim dissidents. All these helped to get me blacklisted. My air travel to the region had become increasingly colorful with incidents of being secondaried and detained, though no longer than overnight in the worst case. I was stuck out there on the skyline, as the saying goes.

CIA was quick to agree to my moving from State to the White House, and my interviews with Condi Rice and Steven Hadley went smoothly. The Saudis were equally quick to bark themselves blue over it. Bandar was so argumentative in his opposition that it further dimmed my assessment of his fitness for his job. He alleged to US officials that I had written flattering things about Bin Laden and wanted to damage the US-Saudi relationship. Not only was he transparently lying, but did he not appreciate that a director was on the lowest rung at the NSC? But he did not give up, and eventually, the NSC had second thoughts about me.

"Well," Elliott told me apologetically a few weeks later, "I guess it's fair to ask whether you can be effective in your job if the major country in your account is dead set against working with you. I'll tell Condi we might have to rethink this. In a few months, the North Africa directorship will open up—think about whether you'd want to take that on."

How I wish I had been at the Senior Directors meeting in the West Wing later that week when he did bring it up. Condi asked, "Where are we on your Persian Gulf director?" and Elliott responded that the Saudis were unrelenting in their opposition to me. They had raised it with Deborah Jones and several others at State; now we had a problem. And then, down the length of the table, other senior directors—Otto Reich, who was Western Hemisphere; Dan Fried, who was Europe; Cindy Courville, who was Africa—all chimed in. Yes, indeed, Bandar had called them, too. The consensus was that the Saudis were unhappy and digging in. Condi was appalled at the brazenness of the Saudis' lobbying and declared that the White House could not even have the appearance of a foreign government interfering in our staffing. "Please tell Peter the job is his," she told Elliott.

The job was mine, pending the results of the mandatory drug test, anyway. I could not help gloating as I provided my urine sample at the Interior Department building a couple of blocks down Pennsylvania Avenue. Leave it to Bandar's embassy to hold a grudge, overreact, misread how the US government worked—and thus guarantee my job.

When I asked a predecessor what the hardest part about the White House job was, she told me it was not global crises, but getting clothes dry cleaned. "You work from early morning until night, so forget the work week. You can try for same-day service on Saturdays, but you end up working a lot of Saturdays." And this in a workplace where your suits, shirts, and ties had to be perfect all the time.

A heartening feature of the White House was the lack of the ego and sharp elbows so prevalent at State. You are told early on that the NSC is a presidential staff, and there is only one important person on the "18 acres" (which is the White House compound, including Treasury next door). Everyone hustled to get the work done, making for a highly collaborative environment. Yet despite this teamwork, there were no teams: We worked our accounts on our own, without backup. A day off meant persuading a busy colleague to take on your entire workload.

This happened to me early on. The Iraq director, Phil Remler, needed a weekend off, and I saw no harm in covering for him for a short period involving no weekdays. That Saturday night, I was having dinner at Bamyan, an Afghan restaurant in suburban Herndon, when my work-issued BlackBerry rang and vibrated (I would develop a Pavlovian hatred for the device within hours of receiving it.) It was the White House Situation Room, the 24-hour outfit like the CIA's Operations Center. The caller ascertained that I was the point of contact for Iraq affairs in Mr. Remler's absence and reported that a car bomb in Najaf, Iraq, had just killed Ayatollah Muhammad Baqir al-Hakim. The President would need to send a letter of condolence the next day, and I was to write it. Even tipsy, I knew this drill—composing a full package for the Oval Office: a cover memo to Condi Rice explaining why she needed to pass this to the President (Tab A); a memo to the President offering background on al-Hakim's significance and details of the assassination and repercussions (Tab B); and the draft condolence letter for the President's signature—the first-ever letter from a US president condoling an ayatollah (Tab C).

It was nearly ten PM, and I was pretty hammered in an outer suburb. I gamely suggested to the caller that I would get into the White House first thing in the morning to get this done.

"Just as you say, sir," he replied, "but the Executive Staff will need the completed package by five AM at the latest."

This initiation into the work ethic at 1600 Pennsylvania Avenue saw me disarming the vault in the Executive Office Building a little before midnight and opening my safe—as at State, there was a "clean desk" policy at the NSC. The US mission in Baghdad had released several cables on the event. A double car bombing at the Imam Ali Shrine in Najaf had killed al-Hakim and about a hundred others, including fifteen of his bodyguards. Baathists loyal to Saddam or al-Qa'ida were probably responsible. Career ambassador Hume Horan, a renowned Arabist assigned to Baghdad, earned my eternal gratitude by having supplied an eloquent draft condolence letter. I wrote the package, sent it to the Executive Secretary, secured the vault by three AM, and devoted the next day to drinking coffee, napping, and ironing shirts.

Iran policy was housed chiefly in the Southwest Asia Directorate. It was headed by Zalmay Khalilzad, who invited me to his meetings, mainly relating to Iran's nuclear program, in such numbing scientific detail that if it had been a college course, I would have flunked it. My main takeaway was that Iran wanted a bomb, and the Israelis assessed the Iranians would develop a bomb before we thought they would. Separately, I listened to several varieties of Iranian exiles complain about the Tehran regime, which usually was not time well-spent because they were preaching to the choir and had no solutions; more passionate by far were visitors from the California Pistachio Growers Association, who lamented the Clinton-era exemptions on Iran sanctions to allow Iran products into the US with gestures and facial expressions that would have done silent movie actors proud. Zal passed on those meetings.

The least fun civics lesson in the US government is that the president makes policy, and the cabinet departments implement it. It brings some staffers in the national security departments, like State and Defense, close to despair. Distraught hawks in the administration would share with me their grief and rage that the softies in the State Department kept the Iranian group Mojahedin-Khalq on the terrorism list because they (the distraught) had, in turn, been treated to the grief and rage of the MEK's skeezy, shiny-suited lobbyists who operated out of some barely legal kind of press cover in Washington. I had to explain that a succession of presidents had kept the MEK on the list—entirely their *presidential* prerogative— because it was a desperate cult with a lot of American blood on their hands, even if we fully reciprocated their loathing for their country of origin. State maintained that list at the president's pleasure. But it seems the MEK had revealed to us Tehran's nuclear bomb development activities at Fordo, and that won them a lot of love among some of the hawks.

Similarly, on the other side of the Arabian Gulf, the NSC found ourselves in the sideshow world of hard-working but dovish and big-ego State staffers who were susceptible to the charms of ambassadors from the little Gulf states. I knew the cast of characters from almost daily visits to State's Near East Bureau on my bicycle and everyone's national day receptions (my little Gulfies, but sometimes the Europeans too), the first-tour desk officers who were the smartest people they ever met, and the indolent but endlessly suave diplomats representing the sheikhdoms. One of these ambassador-level charmers brought to mind Diana Vreeland's observation about Clark Gable having the eyelashes of a Shetland pony. A newbie desk officer, enthralled with endless lunches and sweet talk with his excellency, phoned me one day in a near-panic.

"Peter—what have you been telling Bishr (not his real name)?" Lana (not her real name) demanded accusingly, referring to her frequent host Ambassador Bishr, Ambassador of Thanistan (not a real country). "Believe me, he is *not happy*! I had to talk him down for about twenty minutes."

She sounded like an outraged mom scolding me, the neighborhood bully, for pushing her baby boy off a swing set. In fact, Ambassador Eyelashes represented a country whose media produced nonstop propaganda, uniformly conspiratorial and antisemitic against the US and Israel, and highly sympathetic to terrorist groups like al-Qaida and Hezbollah. This was despite, or because of, the diminutive state's cozy relationship with the Pentagon. Eyelashes had a limitless budget to wine and dine our diplomats and generals but got routinely hauled in and lectured by the NSC, who had no time for the wining, dining, propaganda, or suggestive charm.

I reminded Lana, as I impatiently watched dozens of emails cascading into my inbox and the phone lighting up with other incoming calls, that Bishr's tiny country and its eleven citizens were in daily violation of all the diplomatic norms we supposedly agreed on and that we clearly saw their little game of cultivating every friend and enemy to save their plutocratic skins, and were not amused by it. I reminded her for the dozenth time that if Bishr was getting mixed messages from the White House and from her (whose love of Prosecco and Wagyu beef he knew well), he should figure out which message was the valid one. Her job, I repeated, was to represent US policy, whether she liked it or not.

"So what am I supposed to *do*?" she almost shouted. This bold challenge was, of course, just a juvenile proclamation that she was unfit for her job—yet, anyway. I think she has since made ambassador somewhere.

Culture beats organization in Washington as in Hollywood (ask Lynda Obst), and the lifers in the policy world often did outlive the revolving-door tribe who were their supposed superiors. An anecdote from the Reagan years, which my boss Elliott Abrams related, was a case study in how the system was designed to work instead. Reagan took office when Bulgaria, ruled by dictator Todor Zhivkov, was the Soviet Union's most reliable satellite, and the US, as a result, had no ambassador accredited to

Sofia. Reagan and Secretary of State George Schutz had to decide—keep relations cool and low-level to remind Sofia of our displeasure or send in an ambassador who would send a clear message? They took the latter course and sent a youngish career diplomat, Mel Levitzky, as ambassador to Soviet Premier Andropov's favorite Warsaw Bloc lapdog.

At the ceremony in 1984 where Zhivkov welcomed Levitsky to present his ambassadorial credentials, the Bulgarian expressed the boilerplate wish that this would mean an era of improved US-Bulgarian relations.

"Improving US-Bulgarian relations is not my job," Levitzky informed the startled despot. "My job is to advance the national security interests of the United States. That might mean improving relations, or it might mean damaging them."

That is how you talk to our foreign frenemies, eyelashes or not.

At the NSC, I thought back to the CIA officers who sheepishly admitted that the first week they started the job, they sought ways to search databases for secrets about the Kennedy assassination or UFOs in New Mexico. Now, granted access to the even more restricted White House files, I was on the hunt for the written correspondence between heads of state and the transcripts of their phone calls (called "telcons," these were the fastidious work of the White House Situation Room staff, who scheduled and transcribed the conversations).

These were enthralling—intense, brainy, and, given the busy schedules of the US President and his peers, blunt. Foreign leaders brought their gossip A game to their time with the leader of the free world to titillate, hold his attention, or demonstrate their global access to secrets. The unique classification marking was "Confidential President's Eyes Only." "Eyes only" meant no one could share these outside the building; protected by executive privilege, they would not end up in places where they might be unearthed in a Freedom of Information Act (FOIA) request. The light "Confidential" marking, on the other hand, enabled declassification for these crown jewels of sensitivity for use in a chatty presidential memoir. I can't quote them here, but you can check out bestsellers, *Decision Points* by George W. Bush, and *A Promised Land* by Barack Obama.

And there were some materials with no apparent US government connection. By far the most poignant of these, orphaned in an unnumbered manila folder and lacking any trace of origin or follow-on action, was a fawning letter from former President of the Soviet Union Mikhail Gorbachev to a Saudi Arabian prince. The latter was a patron of a few progressive causes such as the environment and, as a royal well within the vast *highness* category (versus the narrow *royal highness* caste at the highest altitude of the ruling family), his name would probably not ring a bell with you. The date of Gorbachev's letter placed it squarely in the waning days of his Social

Democratic Party of Russia (Putin was consolidating power), and he sent it from Western Europe, where he recounted a meeting with a duchess who, he wrote, had urged him to make his political capital available to the prince.

Written in competent English, the former Soviet premier's missive ridiculously addressed his target as "Your Royal Highness" and pleaded a desperate interest in the prince's ecological projects, which were close to his heart. He proclaimed himself available to fly to Riyadh at a moment's notice. He eagerly awaited a favorable response. He signed himself your devoted etc., Mikhail Sergeyevich etc.

I tried to imagine the meeting Gorbachev cited, which might have taken place in Luxembourg. An on-the-ropes Russian politician and a clapped-out duchess—maybe Russian as well?—had a heart-to-heart talk about where's the money these days? She has come to know a Saudi prince, maybe slept with him, and wants to make herself useful to the former leader of the USSR. Mikhail Sergeyevich is all over the Green Party cause, which succeeded communism in biting the ankles of capitalism. He has a stab at getting petrodollars for the Gorbachev Foundation, already being co-opted and hollowed out by his adversaries. In vain.

This was all just my pure speculation, of course. There was no sign of any Saudi response to Gorbachev, but *someone* passed his letter to a US president—a form of gossip—to illustrate how far the Russian had fallen. Or ... in the spirit of *Maybe you can help this guy?* I'm not naming the prince because he must have been the source. How else did this sad *billet-doux* end up in my file cabinet?

Meanwhile, the Saudis had finally started to "get it" on terrorism, thanks to car bombs, which by 2003 had started to blow up police stations and other regime targets. Al-Qa'ida had long gone after foreign targets in Saudi Arabia—well after the September 11 attacks—yet the government was still unmotivated to solve this problem they had so much to do with creating. Regime preservation was something they understood, however, and so the touchy tribal Arab, who lived for a good vendetta, had finally awoken in them, though it would take about two years before they grasped the extent of the threat and were able to counter it.

Unfortunately, Saudi misbehavior was not limited to suicidal young fanatics. The Saudi Embassy in Washington was a mess. Its movements of huge amounts of cash, including to highly subsidized Saudi students in the US, left it open to (baseless) suspicions that it had funded the September 11 attackers. We suspected it had many out-of-status diplomats still residing in the US. Its sponsorship of anti-Jewish and anti-Christian incitement through propaganda had not ceased. Bandar was doing the main thing expected of every ambassador: maintaining excellent access to the highest levels of our government. When it came to the day-to-day management of his embassy, though, he and Rihab may have missed a few things.

It was at about this time that Condi brought in a New York prosecutor, Frances Fragos Townsend, as Assistant to the President for Homeland Security and Counterterrorism. Much as I was not personally gunning for the Saudis (*pace* Prince Bandar), I loved how Fran introduced herself. "In New York, I shut down the Gambinos. Down here, you and I are going to fix the Saudis."

Over the weeks and months, we summoned Rihab and asked for an accounting of all Saudi embassy personnel in the United States, including all its consulates. Any US ambassador could supply this kind of information about a mission's staff and their dependents in fifteen minutes. The Saudis asked for a week, then a month, and then delayed indefinitely as they hurried to figure out who was out of status to send them home before we could expel them. We learned of diplomatic passport holders in the oddest places, and of many out-of-status embassy vehicles. The Saudis maintained the second-largest motor pool in Washington after the Russians. We worked with State Protocol to change the digraph on their diplomatic plate from KV to LN, so that the mandatory swapping of license plates would force all their vehicles into status.

Separately, the FBI had been investigating the Saudi-sponsored Institute for the Islamic and Arabic Studies in America (IIASA), located in Arlington, Virginia. Prince

Bandar was the chairman of its board but probably paid it as little attention as he paid to anything his embassy did. On the morning of July 2, 2004, FBI agents, customs officers, and IRS showed up at IIASA with search warrants and spent all day and much of the evening removing hard drives, collecting paperwork, and emptying its mailroom, which was the origin of much of the Saudi hate literature that made it way to mosques and prison chaplains. The diplomatic visas of eleven of its staff would be revoked. This was on top of sixteen Saudi diplomats expelled from the US as part of our effort to clean up their embassy.

The IIASA raid was a purely law enforcement matter, but Bandar could not believe it was not orchestrated by Fran and me. Not long after the IIASA raid, Condi phoned me to say that the President's father had called her from Kennebunkport to report that Prince Bandar had contacted him asking to visit the ex-president in Maine. Bandar gave no reason for wanting to visit, so Bush asked Condi if she knew anything; she didn't and directed me to call Rihab to find out. I did, and he assured me that there was no agenda. Bush needed no advance information for the warm, familial conversation Bandar hoped to have with him and the former first lady. And so Bandar flew to Kennebunkport, then to Jackson Hole, where Vice President Cheney was vacationing, and back to DC, where he went to see Tenet.

Bandar had one message for all three: Frances Townsend and Peter Theroux were undermining the vital Saudi-US relationship and had to be reined in. The bewildered ex-president in Maine had no idea who Bandar was talking about and could offer no help. Cheney told him that Fran was not malicious and, since the Veep had his own bloated staff to manage, he probably had no clue who I was either. Tenet was blunt, telling Bandar that Fran enjoyed the President's full confidence and advised him to learn to get along with her, fast. And Peter was CIA, so leave him alone. Bandar, who must have thought we were all stupid or did not talk to each other, then magnanimously invited Fran to his grand residence in McLean for drinks to tell her, "You know, you've pissed me off, but I'm going to overlook it." Of course, the despised Director of Persian Gulf Affairs was not invited.

The Arabs call it the Arabian Gulf, and their ambassadors were always taking me to task over my title. The Iran-hating Saudis were especially touchy about those little pasteboard cards in my pocket with the word *Persian* on them. There was nothing about me they did not hate. This always cheered me up when I was feeling low, much as it probably cheered them up that I was about to be sent to a warzone.

THE DESTRUCTION OF SENNACHERIB

In 2004, I was sent to Iraq as an aide to Bob Blackwill. A former ambassador to India, Blackwill had been named the NSC's Senior Director for Iraq, and he would be traveling there as the US special envoy to join the UN envoy, Lakhdar Brahimi, who was already in country. They were to work with the Iraqis to stand up their first post-Saddam government as the US-led Coalition Provisional Authority was stood down. I had an affinity for Iraq and the Iraqis but had resisted this assignment because of Blackwill's reputation as a brilliant but abusive old party. Elliott argued to the West Wing for me that I was needed at home and that my portfolio already touched on Iraq and Iran policy, but there was no avoiding my turn. No other White House staffer who had traveled with Blackwill was willing to repeat the experience. Bob's "hall file" went back as far as the 1960s, when he served in the Peace Corps in East Africa with my brother Paul, who remembered him as an insufferable know-it-all even then, at age twenty-two. (The American administrating the Coalition Provisional Authority [CPA] in Iraq, Paul Bremer, had been a junior officer in the US Embassy in Malawi when Paul and Blackwill were PCVs there—the world's a shoebox, as the Aussies say.) In the event, I found that he was indeed the most disagreeable bastard I ever worked with in government, even if a beer or two did change his demeanor entirely for the better. One night at the palace in Baghdad, he drank some beer and was trying to remember what came after "The Assyrian came down like a wolf on the fold," and when I supplied the next few lines from the Byron poem, he crowed, "I knew you were a literary man!" and behaved kindly for more than an hour. The next day, he was back to giving preposterous orders and responding to my hesitation with, "Stop trying to wrap your big fucking brain around this and do as you're told!"

Before the insurgency or civil war began—fueled by Baathist dead-enders, the always malevolent Iranians, and their Syrian Baathist allies—post-Saddam Iraq was peaceful and optimistic, though the internal dynamics of the CPA were a mess. The commanding general of the Coalition, Rick Sanchez, and Bremer made no secret of their (well-documented) loathing for each other. Bremer wanted to be an ambassador. Blackwill saw himself as a kingmaker and, despite his immense book smarts, was by far the dumbest of the three. (See my ten Rules at the end of this book—he violated all of them.) Sanchez, the product of a poor, pious, and macho Mexican-American culture, understood poor, pious, and macho Iraq perfectly and was fearless in overruling his supposed political over-lords. (He knew the Rules well.)

Once the new Iraqi government was in place, I told Blackwill I quit; the Agency wanted me to stay on in Baghdad a little while in a different capacity, and I had easily obtained the West Wing's buy-in—Blackwill was so widely loathed that it was a cinch to undermine him, especially among his own NSC staff. Of course, he cursed, spat nails, and threatened, "I'll go to Condi on this!" giving me the pleasure of informing him that Condi had already agreed to let me separate from his testy little mission.

To the surprise of no one, Blackwill would later get canned from State for physically abusing an employee.

My brother Paul commented that it was fitting for a bastard second only to Jimmy Swaggart for sporting a villainous name straight out of a Dickens novel.

Back in Washington, Condi was moving on to become Secretary of State, and Steve Hadley moved up to replace her. Steve and I got along well, and he offered to extend me another year at the White House. Truthfully, I was exhausted, and in my time there, I had learned the policy world well enough to be better at intelligence work, which is what I liked better and missed. I offered to stay six more months, but the timing was tricky—the 2004 elections would be turbulent and time-consuming "downtown," (this time designating the executive branch). So we agreed I would head back to Headquarters after completing one last task: designating Saudi Arabia, one of the countries violating religious freedoms. It should have always been on the list, as it enforced a ban on all non-Muslim worship and even constrained Shia Muslim observances. This was no more a private score of mine to settle than the IIASA raid was; it had finally gotten traction because religious freedom, along with Latin American affairs, Middle East peace, and human rights, were all strong suits of Elliott's. And because not doing it would have been ridiculous. The Department of State complied and justified the list on behalf of the White House, but since it had the day-to-day chore of diplomacy with the governments we were listing, they tended to go wobbly when told to add anyone to it.

Predictably, State pushed back ("What's changed?"), but the thoughtful US Ambassador in Riyadh, James Oberwetter ("Obi" to President Bush), was realistic, if mildly reluctant. When I mentioned this gambit to him on the phone, he said, "I don't think it's the time for this. Having said that, I don't think any time will be an easy time for it. I don't look forward to giving this news to King Abdallah. If it's the President's wish, do it."

I understood the spot he was in. Despite Saudi Arabia's blatant religious intolerance, Bush and Abdallah had a close personal rapport, established amid the Second Intifada, but even so, Abdallah was enraged at Bush's pro-Israel views and threatened to cut short his visit to the presidential ranch in Texas; Abdallah even referred to Israeli Prime Minister Ariel Sharon as a "pig." Bush wrote about this in his memoirs. (Once, in an Oval Office conversation, Bush told this story and added, looking straight at me, "You do not come to my fucking ranch and call my friend a pig.") At that precarious low point, Bush and Abdallah had a famous heart-to-heart talk in a drive around the ranch, accompanied only by an interpreter, much to the chagrin of the Secret Service; POTUS out of their sight and control with an unpredictable Arab was an unwelcome security novelty, as was POTUS driving himself. A rebuff to the kingdom now might undo some of the newly minted goodwill. I suggested to Oberwetter that since a lot of Saudi religious fanatics were unhappy about Abdallah's closeness to the US government, this move might boost Abdallah's credibility domestically, especially among the clerical class, for US complaints that Abdallah was hard on the infidels would greatly hearten them. The ambassador took it on board, as they say at State, and the designation went through.

Headquarters felt like home. Now assigned to the Counterterrorism Center, I was working ten-hour days instead of fifteen-hour days, was relieved of policy pre-scriptions, and had the leisure time to start translating a novel, Elias Khoury's *Yalo*. The transition from the White House office to a tiny workstation in CTC was therapeutic, even blissful, as I shed the policymaker ego and started to "get smart," as they said, on al-Qa'ida, which was especially restive in Iraq, Jordan, and Saudi Arabia. The tempo of ter-rorist attacks in Saudi Arabia was especially striking, with successive bombings and massacres targeting non-Muslim foreigners. The religious establishment occasionally found words of regret for the shedding of blood on Saudi soil of those who were entitled to protection, meaning that, technically speaking, the massacres were bad manners because the foreigners were present in the country legally. They could not condemn the murders outright because that would go against the preaching every Friday against Crusaders, Zionists, infidels, and polytheists. It brought me back to a White House conversation with Bandar, when he was asked why Riyadh was not more forceful against the long-bearded extremists and the imams inciting violence.

"That's our constituency," he said, with awkward candor, then immediately started to backtrack.

In the meantime, Iraq was looking grim. Jordanian-born terrorist Abu Mus'ab al-Zarqawi had emerged as a full-blown psychotic who hated Shia Muslims as much as he hated non-Muslims and was as busy blowing up Shia mosques as he was kidnapping and beheading Americans. Even his fellow al-Qa'ida members were afraid of him. Amidst the other mayhem, in late March 2004, four American contractors were murdered in Fallujah, Iraq, their bodies dismembered and burned; this was al-Qaida's work. Most of the terrorists were non-Iraqis, entering Iraq from Syria through the notorious FFP or Foreign Fighter Pipeline, enabled from Damascus Airport to Iraq's western border by the Syrian government. A huge disproportion of them were Tunisians. The Syrian regime shared an aspiration with the Iranian one: to make the American experience in Iraq so painful that we would never attempt regime change again. At the White House, Elliott had argued in vain for the bombing of Damascus Airport.

I was about to get much closer to this problem because the US intelligence effort in Iraq had a senior vacancy no one was eager to fill. It was a management job, as the DI had sent many analysts and targeters to support the military coalition and various embassy functions, and someone had to shape the overall effort. I had never aspired to management, particularly in a warzone, but I was asked to go to Baghdad for a few months to help out. Of all my qualifications for the assignment, I think the strongest was that I had not had a chance to settle deeply into my Headquarters slot, so there was no cost, in terms of the analytic CT mission, to subtracting me. My NSC mission to Iraq with Blackwill had confined me to the palace and on VIP airlift around the country, given Blackwill's seniority. My role in this new capacity would expose me more, so I was hastily put through trauma responder and counterintelligence training, certified on the M4 rifle and Glock 9-millimeter pistol, and put on a plane.

Baghdad was familiar to me from two visits I had made long before government service, so navigating the city and the varieties of Iraqi Arabic were easy to pick up again. The cultural adjustment wasn't from the American to the Mesopotamian capital, but from Headquarters, where analysts mostly spoke to other analysts, to the field, where we spoke to operators, targeters, American and foreign diplomats, a whole range of host-country players, and officers from the Coalition militaries: British, Danish, Salvadoran, Gurkhas, and a dozen more. The stovepipes were demolished, a mostly healthy development. And Washington, especially my time downtown at the NSC, had taught me some diplomacy for friendlies and thick skin for the others.

Any doubts about the Baghdad job not being a challenge were dispelled my first morning when I attended the management meeting, addled from jet lag and hoping for a few friendly introductions and a short day to start learning the job. The evening prior, upon arrival, my new boss had briefly sketched it out. "I run a warfighting effort here, and I have no time for analysts. That whole thing is yours. Don't come to me with any decision you can make on your own." He opened his palms vertically and pushed them at me like dumping an invisible burden into my lap.

The first item of business was a certain terrorist who was behind a particularly appalling string of car bombings against Shia targets: mosques, schools, and the funerals of those killed by previous attacks. Overnight intelligence revealed that he was an Iraqi in his early twenties who was studying for his master's degree and running a car bomb factory in a Baghdad slum.

"I am officially sick and tired of this asshole," my new boss announced. "If we cannot stop this punk, what the fuck good are we, or our mighty coalition?" He looked directly at me and the ops officer beside me. "Get to work on this guy. This should not take long."

"Got it," I said calmly, horrified. This would mean pulling together the targeting analysts, the signals experts, and many others to develop a targeting package full of sensitive intelligence that would need to be cleared for release to the other Coalition countries we would involve, primarily the Iraqis. Ridiculously, a FISA[4] warrant would be needed if the terrorist was using US technology like Yahoo messaging; we would have to figure out his pattern of life,

---

[4] The Nixon-era Foreign Intelligence Surveillance Act protected Americans from US espionage activities. It also meant that foreign terrorists using things like Yahoo Messenger or US area code numbers enjoyed protection from us, until we obtained a warrant.

locate him, and prepare for his capture and debriefing. This was intimidating in my first half-hour on the job. To buy time and elicit some specific guidance, I asked, "Chief, to turn the right resources on to this guy, want to give me any sense of what we're willing to turn off? I imagine we're flat-out against every target already." I loved how thoughtful I sounded.

"Gee, and here I was thinking I had a fucking deputy who could figure out shit like that for himself," he replied. Colleagues had warned me of this man's great bullshit detector, and he also recognized flailing when he saw it. The warzone was truly nothing like what field officers called "Hindquarters." In the following days, the case started with targeting analysts and was briskly moved over to operators and the military for execution.

Fortunately, our target loved chatting on his phone as much as he loved murdering innocent people. Within the week, he was tracked driving into central Baghdad and over the July 14 Bridge. The bridge was quickly closed on both ends, Polish and US troops on one side and Iraqis on the other. He was still chatting on the phone when he was pulled out of his car. I don't know his fate, but as our operators say, when you have to choose, call 1-800-FLOWERS.

It was far easier to adapt to the pace of Baghdad than to that of the White House. At home, there was the futility of trying to keep up with friends and family, buy food, iron shirts, and otherwise try to maintain normality. There was no shred of social life in this war zone except for mealtimes, no distractions, no family, and very little downtime—recreational time was mostly confined to the gym and shooting range. We wanted to stay alive and do our jobs from early morning until late at night. There was no sign of the problems that had deterred me from taking a management job at home—whiny analysts, budgets, editing other people's work. Overwork or homesickness here represented serious vulnerabilities and required real problem-solving skills. The counterintelligence lessons we learned in the haunted woods of Washington had a whole new altitude of meaning when Iranians and al-Qa'ida were all around us, and the stupid analyst tricks we chuckled about at home were a serious concern here when the analysts were carrying firearms they barely knew how to use. Bad judgment here could get someone, and many more, killed. On the other hand, praise, encouragement, learning how to convey orders, and being an attentive listener here went a long way to build morale.

Walking home to my tiny trailer at night, under the big yellow moon through the palm trees, with bats zigzagging up and down the night sky, I felt immensely fulfilled. My last goodnights were always with the soldiers of the Hawaii Army National Guard who protected us. From within their quarters, you could usually overhear their twentieth screening of the day of the satirical movie "Team America: World Police." The soldiers could shout along with nearly every line of dialogue and the songs, and after a few months, so could I.

Nothing in "Team America" outdid the absurdity and tempo of visiting Congressional delegations. After the merest professional conversations with us, they wanted to go shopping and pose for photo-ops with deployed military from their states, no matter how remote in Iraq or the cost to Coalition airlift. The most colorful were Joe Biden, Carl Levin, and Curt Weldon. (Trust me, I could keep you here all day.)

My acerbic boss eventually took a moderate liking to me, or as much of one as was possible for someone whose management philosophy was "the lack of a stick is the carrot." He liked using me as his interpreter, as many of our excellent Arabic interpreters—"terps"—came from all kinds of Middle Eastern backgrounds and so lacked fluency in the Iraqi dialects. My ease with the language won praise, sometimes lavish, from the Arabs my boss engaged with. When my five months were up, and my permanent replacement arrived—let's call him Skip—he took a dim view of Skip. Skip was a lightweight, but at least he committed to a year in Baghdad when no one wanted to come here. I dearly wanted to get on the chopper to BIAP (Baghdad Airport, which I had first known as Saddam Hussein International) and then home. I urged Skip to bond with the boss, in vain. Skip was afraid of him.

"I'm inclined to send him home. You need to stay here," the boss told me, standing outside our workplace one evening, having summoned me with a crook of his index finger. "He doesn't know anything about this country, and he can't speak Arabic."

This reminded me of a recent brush with risk brought about by my interpreting work. One of our Arab interlocutors, known to be friendly with Iraq's neighbors to the east, had approached me at a reception and regaled a hard-featured friend of his with flattering accounts of my language abilities, which, he swore, put me in the one percent of westerners who truly understood the region. This led into a sprightly series of questions of almost indecent specificity, which seemed to come naturally to his friend. Counterintelligence was not my strong suit, but I had Lynda Obst to warn me: "Beware of obsequious human beings. Everyone here has a strong, healthy ego. (Natural selection requires it.) The most dangerous wolves are in sheep's clothing." I changed the subject to the weather and made a note to observe the two-man rule at future receptions. And hmm, might I cite issues like this as a justification to leave the country? Play it safe—the enemies had a bead on me.

But there was no changing the subject with my boss. Even knowing he might sense more flailing on my part, I made my case. I was only here TDY (temporary duty), and Skip was here PCS, on a permanent change of station assignment. He was a good guy and would grow on him and should be given a chance. At least those were the rules from Hindquarters.

"Nice try. You know I can keep you here in TDY status for eleven months and twenty-nine days after I send his narrow ass home, right? Talk to him."

I talked to Skip as only someone grimly determined to leave Iraq could. A few times a day, I walked past the posted flight manifest with my name on it, and it read like poetry.

Unpronounceable Locations

I am going to word this very carefully now because the next field assignments I got far outdid the Iraqi one in sensitivity, were far more consequential, and probably still have the power to complicate my family life. The sibling who called me a "two-dollar whore" for agreeing to work in the Bush White House still does not know about them, so I will be vague as well, thinking ahead to the Prepublication Review Board as well as siblings who are know-it-alls about what they call torture. (If you are reading this, we made it through the PRB.)

At a certain point in the War on Terror, the US government began capturing al-Qa'ida members, including some senior ones, and interrogated them. This caused controversy in the media, and civil libertarian groups and the Council of Europe denounced what the US was doing. Even former FBI officials such as Ali Soufan claimed that they knew better and that "torture doesn't work." Torture does not work, but the CIA did not engage in torture, except in aberrant cases where the abusive miscreant was punished. Having relevant language and regional experience, I was asked to go into training as a debriefer of terrorists. This did not involve interrogation and had nothing to do with the misbehavior of Maryland Army

National Guard military police at Abu Ghraib Prison near Baghdad, which the bozos immortalized in photos.

I beam within a few blocks of my first unpronounceable work location, which no longer exists there. Nor does the one described in this chapter.

Interviewing these terrorists in custody, I was instructed, was purely a matter of collecting intelligence. It was neither a privilege nor a punishment for a detainee to be questioned. The questions were not random; they were provided by headquarters analysts who were deeply versed in each detainee's personal and professional activities. They were also provided by our foreign liaison partners, who shared none of their politicians' distaste for our program. The number of detainees in custody meant that we would not be misled by any one of them who wanted to lie, withhold information, fabricate, or embellish. We could ask a dozen detainees the same questions, separately and independently, and see where their accounts differed or aligned, just as police question suspects separately. And since, as with suspects being questioned separately, they knew their peers were also being questioned, which motivated them not to lie.

Further, al-Qa'ida members had their own expertise about the program. Once they learned that one of their number had been captured, they deemed all his operations to be compromised and canceled them. They tracked who was captured and in what order. When a detainee being debriefed seemed to detect skepticism on my face, he would say things like, "Ask Abu Zubayda! Ask Hawsawi—they were there!" I would not respond but would be thinking, "Of course I'm going to ask him in about an hour because he's down the hall. Or my colleague in Country X already has."

Even when telling the truth, or as little of it as they calculated they could get away with, the terrorists were repulsive and resented being losers. We stayed impervious. Analysts who already prided themselves on their objectivity were further trained and scrutinized for bias and mental stability. If you were facing the mastermind of the September 11 attacks or some other creep, you could be neither intimidated nor enraged. We were always polite and professional in our questioning. We were not to say please or thank you. or I'm sorry, but we could smile. We were closely watched by guards in the room and monitored by cameras in real time. All of the terrorists were easy to dislike, but some of them showed humor or neediness. If any felt contrition, I never saw it. They liked boasting and being helpful. Their debriefing sessions were a break from sitting in their rooms, and we gave them treats and snacks as well as paper cups of tea, lukewarm rather than hot, in case they should decide to throw it at us.

I had one near disaster and many successes in this line of work. The near disaster occurred because I spoke Arabic. This was a rare occurrence because all debriefing was done in English, with an interpreter if one was needed, unless someone else in the room or doing the monitoring also understood the detainee's mother tongue. A one-on-one conversation, in which the debriefer was the single point of failure, was not allowed. Our detainee, from a Levantine country, was comfortably seated, one wrist cuffed to an iron ring in the floor, answering questions about his numerous failed attempts to get into al-Qa'ida before he finally succeeded in swearing loyalty to the group. He described one particularly clumsy incident that cost him credibility.

"Kharjak," I commented. This expression—"Serves you right"—is very common in Levantine Arabic. It was the kind of lighthearted colloquial remark we were allowed to make to build rapport and make elicitation easier without praising or intimidating a detainee.

He froze and fell silent, and tears started streaming

down his cheeks. The guards took notice and stared at me. The detainee then started heaving and sobbing loudly, his head bowed, wiping away the tears with his free hand. Aware of the various sets of eyes trained at that moment, not on him but on me, I repressed a vivid feeling of panic. All of them, including me and the other Arabic speaker, were thinking *What the fuck!*

The detainee pulled himself together, and I reached for the right unapologetic words to move us along.

"Are you all right? I do not know what I said that upset you."

"It's fine," he said. "I haven't heard that expression since I was a small boy. When I got into trouble, my dad would tell me *kharjak,* and then he'd kiss me and forgive me. I was just thinking of back when I was an innocent kid. I'm sorry. Please ask me some more questions."

They could say they were sorry even if we couldn't. We moved along in the interview, and later that day, I felt like a detainee myself as I sat down with my colleagues and walked them through the conversation, answered some testy questions, and sparred over whether I needed to be sent home for having subjected a detainee to emotional abuse. I was not sent home. That detainee was eventually released—not to his home country, which did not want him—and resumed murdering people.

And then a modest success. A NATO ally—let us say it was France because it was definitely not France—passed us a photograph from a street camera of a young man with a clear full-face view, maybe in his early twenties, wearing a backpack and a sweet smile. They thought he might be al-Qa'ida but did not say why. Might we please see if any detainees recognized him? They welcomed in advance the promptest sharing of anything we learned. This was typical of the Europeans—while their politicians, media, and civil libertarians were denouncing us, their intelligence services lined up around the block asking our help to help protect their populations—typically, requesting information from us while sharing nothing about their boy.

We altered the background and other details of the photo to fuzz the context for the photo-recognition exercise, and we also selected a dozen other dummy photos of random faces. I then started my rounds of detainees to find out if any of them recognized him— my tenth or eleventh "photo rec."

One after another, the detainees denied knowing any of them. Then, one and another paused at our Frenchman and said they had met him. I went through the usual questions. When? Where? Who else was there? What did he say? What did he do? And so on.

One detainee remembered him well, making a total of five terrorists in detention who had had eyes on the fellow in the photo. He said that this youth had arrived in an Afghan city at a specific time and had a meeting. He stayed for only one night before being sent on to Khaldan Camp, Abu Zubayda's camp, which meant training to be a suicide bomber. Did you see him again? *No, he left*

Afghanistan by another way. Did you talk to him? *Yes.* In what language? *French.* I asked, how good was his French? *Fluent,* I was told, *like any Parisian.* I asked, very carefully, do you mean he had native fluency? Or that he spoke in a specifically Parisian dialect? *Oh,* he answered, *a perfectly Parisian accent, like any native.* In response to follow-up questions, he named other people who had been in the meeting and who had said what.

There are four levels of precedence for a cable: Routine, Priority, Immediate, and NIACT, which means night action—someone will be hauled out of bed to read it. That night, from the remote town on an unnamed continent where our site was located, I rousted both Headquarters and our NATO ally with a NIACT cable alerting them that, based on firsthand reporting corroborated by multiple credible sources, this winsome, beardless young man roaming their country was an al-Qa'ida-trained suicide bomber. In the weeks and months that followed, no suicide attack occurred in that country. Presumably, the NATO ally found, tried, and imprisoned the boy or deported him. I saw no follow-up reporting on our success in any channel. I shrugged and thought, for the hundredth time: *You're welcome.*

While we learned an enormous amount about al-Qa'ida's workings from the detainees, it was rare to get current threat reporting like this, given how dated their information was. Valid threat information was scarce in general.

One of my witty CTC colleagues had developed what

he called "Top Ten Craplousiness Indicators" of intelligence reporting likely to be worthless. Three of them were "1. Threat reporting from the Russians, 2. Threat reporting from the Palestinians, 3. All threat reporting." (Another maxim, borne out by subsequent history, was "Belgium is Waziristan.")[5]

Speaking of lists.

1. Don't call it Langley—none of us do.

2. Agency officers are not "CIA agents." CIA officers collect intel from the foreign agents recruited to provide it.

3. Murphy was an optimist.

4. Lull them into a sense of complacency. *Them* is everyone. You never want to make yourself interesting to anyone—an adversary, a psychologist, a polygrapher. Another version: "Be beige."

5. Build in opportunity, but use it sparingly. This is Tony Mendez (*Argo*) and it means have a Plan B, C, and D. Experienced officers crush crises. Lacking the backlist of crises faced and solved, novices melt down. You might survive, but your reputation won't.

---

5 Pakistan's most notorious terrorist safehaven.

6. Don't harass the opposition. This is Mendez again, a variant on Rule 4 and a rare tenet advising passivity versus offense. Or as Obst puts it: "If you feel compelled to suggest something to a director, think three times. Be sure you're right, and then say it to someone else."

7. Once is an accident, twice is a coincidence, three times is an enemy action.

8. There is no limit to a human being's ability to rationalize the truth.

9. Technology will always let you down.

10. Trust women's instincts. I don't believe in female intuition as such, but I do think that women who have experienced marriage—even more, years of raising toddlers and teenagers, who are natural liars—have the most highly developed sense of skepticism (the number-one quality in intelligence work: You accept nothing at face value). They tend to seek out more context and detail to find the threat, the agenda, the pattern. A female colleague of mine has a darker explanation: "It's a survival instinct. We've been prey all our lives."

End of Part One

Portrait of Peter Theroux by Don Bachardy, August, 1996
© Don Bachardy. Courtesy of Craig Krull Gallery.

P ETER THEROUX IS the author of *Sandstorms: Days and Nights in Arabia, Translating LA,* and *The Strange Disappearance of Imam Moussa Sadr,* and the translator of a dozen novels from Arabic, including *Children of the Alley* by Nobel laureate Naguib Mahfouz and the *Cities of Salt* trilogy by Abdelrahman Munif. His work has been published in Vanity Fair, National Geographic Magazine, the New York Times (before they sucked), the Chicago Tribune, and the Tablet. He served in the US government for over twenty years as an intelligence officer focusing on terrorism and the Middle East and was awarded the Career Intelligence Medal on retirement.